Forty Days on the Mountain with God

Devotionals from the Sermon on the Mount

THE HOLY BIBLE, NEW INTERNATIONAL VERSION®,
NIV® Copyright © 1973, 1978, 1984, 2011 by Biblica, Inc.™
Used by permission. All rights reserved worldwide.

Ronnie L. Worsham

ISBN: 150039596X
ISBN 13: 9781500395964

Cover by Matt Clark

Dedication: To my four wonderful kids, Brandon, Kale, Casey, and Brianna, the ones who so often were my motivation and strength to get up and go back up the mountain one more day. Although grown up now, they are all still constant inspirations to me in my challenge to climb God's mountain.

Contents

Introduction

(Matt 5:1-2)

*Now when he saw the crowds, he went up on a mountainside and sat
down. His disciples came to him, and he began to teach them, saying...*

Some of the most important events in the history of humanity's
relationship with God have happened on mountains. It was on a
mountain that Moses met with God after Israel crossed the Red
Sea. It was on this same mountain that Moses was given the Ten
Commandments and that he was transfigured, as Jesus would
later be. It was on a mountain that Elijah showed who was really
God (Jehovah) and who was *not* really God (the idol, Baal). It
was on a mountain that Jesus, accompanied by Peter, James, and
John, met Moses and Elijah and was transfigured. It was there
that God spoke his approval of Jesus. And as Matthew tells us,
it was on a mountain that Jesus delivered his most famous and
transforming message, the Sermon on the Mount.

Many have found a sense of being closer with God on moun-
taintops. While most of us cannot easily or quickly ascend a
mountain on a daily basis, all of us can figuratively do so in our
moments of solitude with God. This book is designed to aid in
just such an experience. By considering some thoughts about
Jesus, leading up to the text known as the Sermon on the Mount,
and then exploring this sermon of Jesus that was spoken on a

mountain, I believe each one of us can experience the same kind of closeness with God and the same kind of victories as those of old.

May God bless you so that you may bless others.

1

The Man of Galilee

(Matt 3:13-17)

Then Jesus came from Galilee to the Jordan to be baptized by John.
But John tried to deter him, saying, "I need to be baptized by you,
and do you come to me?" Jesus replied, "Let it be so now; it is proper
for us to do this to fulfill all righteousness." Then John consented.
As soon as Jesus was baptized, he went up out of the water. At that
moment heaven was opened, and he saw the Spirit of God descend-
ing like a dove and lighting on him. And a voice from heaven said,
"This is my Son, whom I love; with him I am well pleased."

What is the allure of this Jew who was executed two thousand years ago? We know so very little about him, actually. What is the attraction of this "unattractive" man? "He had no beauty or majesty to attract to him, nothing in his appearance that we should desire him" (Isa 53:2). Why do men and women all over the world seek him out and give their lives to him? Is he just another religious figure gone viral?

The Magi, the wise men from the East, were just the first of countless wise men who came, and come still, from far and wide to seek him (Matt 2:1–2).

The challenge for the Christian is that Christ does not seek to simply influence but rather to reign. He has established a kingdom, with himself as king. However, we humans mostly prefer to be influenced—and only in pleasurable ways. In no way do we want to be reigned over. We do not, in our fleshly natures, completely trust anybody. We want control of our own lives and, as much as possible, that of the world around us. We want to reign. It's the "Tale of the Two Trees," the Tree of Life and the Tree of the Knowledge of Good and Evil (Gen 2 and 3). However, Jesus can only save us if he reigns over us.

Christianity is not just another philosophy among many—it is in fact exclusive of all others. If it is true, then it is not arrogant at all; just reality. If it is not true, it is perhaps the greatest scam in history. People have sought to "tone down" the biblical message, but there is no honesty in such an effort. Christ said, "I am *the* way, *the* truth, and *the* life. No one comes to the Father *except through me*" (John 14:6). He also said he had *all* authority in heaven and on earth (Matt 28:18). Jesus is the one and only king, if he is a king at all.

Is Jesus, as was the child prince in Mark Twain's *The Prince and the Pauper*, dressed as a common child but claiming to be— and acting as if he is—the king? As with Twain's young prince, who had unwittingly been thrust into the harsh world outside the palace, if Jesus really is who he claimed to be, then it is true, no matter who likes it or dislikes it. It is true no matter what seems politically correct at the time. Jesus's way is not (and never was) "comfortable." And until we accept him as king, we are as the unlikely paupers-turned-princes waiting to be crowned king— false kings, in fact, of our own selfish little "kingdoms." Do we do as the young pauper did and admit we are not princes worthy of coronation, letting the real prince step up for it, and letting him esteem us as he wills? Or do we falsely accept the sham coronation of one so unworthy of kingship, even if it is as "kings" of only our own lives?

Jesus either knew something no one else knew, he was an imposter, or he was a sick man. There are no other honest choices, I believe. Some claim he never existed, but it seems there is just too much evidence to the contrary to believe that objectively. Some claim his followers made him out to be something he was not. That is, of course, possible, but why would they maintain such a lie when, rather than benefiting from their testimonies to him, they were mostly forced to suffer and die for their claims? Multiple eyewitnesses, as well as others close to the facts, testified to his claims. Jesus is not just another prophet. He is either the one and only Son from the Father, or he is a hoax. Plain and simple. There is no honest in-between, I believe.

The validity of Christ's claims are asserted by the Apostle Peter in the biblical scriptures:

> And we have the word of the prophets made more certain, and you will do well to pay attention to it, as to a light shining in a dark place [...] For prophecy never had its origin in the will of man, but men spoke from God as they were carried along by the Holy Spirit. (2 Pet 1:19–21)

If it is not all true about him, can any of it really be trusted for spiritual guidance? Either it was "made certain" through the prophecies and their fulfillments, or it was not. You just have to choose, I suppose.

Further, either the Bible is the word of God in some way (or, perhaps better stated, words *from* God), or it is not from God at all. It cannot just be a "good book," since, if that is all it is, it asserts a tremendous lie. God's inspired message is all it ever claims to be, if it is anything at all. How God inspired it and how we are to apply it authoritatively needs careful consideration away from Christian pressure to believe a particular way. But if we believe the scriptures to be inspired in any way, we must not ignore such possibly troubling considerations.

This is where faith comes in. Believing in Jesus leads to believing the Bible, and believing the Bible leads to believing in Jesus. The goal is *life*—spiritual life; the source of that life is God. And Jesus is our source of God. Each has to decide if the evidence supports a belief in the God and the Christ of the Bible. Each must decide if Jesus is the Christ, and if he is to be personally her or his Lord. Each must decide if the Bible is the revelation of God. The whole of the Old Testament seems to me carefully and divinely designed to lead to the conclusion that "Jesus is Lord." The whole of the New Testament seems determined to clearly demonstrate with the stories of his teaching and life that "Jesus is Lord." Certainly, the two combined then leads each of us to decide whether we will live our own lives with Jesus as our Lord. But whatever you decide, you will still have to live by faith. Everyone does. The question is not, "Do you live by faith?" The real question is, "What, or whom, do you live by faith in?" How about you?

The reality is that anything one ends up believing concerning origins, whether about the cosmos in general or about the supernatural in particular, will seem in fact "unbelievable." It just will be. However, something will indeed end up being true. What do you think that is? The truth is not the truth because one believes it. And it is not untrue because one does not. The truth is what simply *is*. The absolute truth is unalterable and unadulterated, even though human thought may skew and obscure it in our own experiences.

As many have observed over the two-plus millennia since Jesus lived, there has never been a greater story ever told. Consider the incredible Old Testament stories and prophecies leading up to Christ. If you will, take some time to pore over the amazingly precise genealogies that track Jesus of Nazareth from the very beginning as the Son of the Promise. Then read on through the stories of John the Baptist who prepared the way for him. Note well Jesus's miraculous birth and obscure infancy. Read about his initiation into his ministry through his baptism by John, when the heavens opened and God's Spirit descended on him like a dove. Hear in your own mind the voice of affirmation from God himself—"This is my Son, whom I love; with him I am well pleased" (Matt 3:17). Observe that miracle follows miracle, so many that his disciple and dear friend, the Apostle

John, concluded his own gospel explaining that Jesus had done so many amazing things that there was not enough room in the world for the books that would be required to record them all (John 21:25). Amazing story follows amazing story. The stories call us not to be entertained or amazed, though; they call us to believe. It challenges us with the supernatural. It challenges us, in fact, with the supranatural. Jesus was from above and beyond, not just better than normal.

"This is my Son, whom I love; with him I am well pleased." The voice from heaven. My Son. Jesus's best friends would later witness the voice of God when the Infinite One said, "This is my Son, whom I love; with him I am well pleased. *Listen to him*" (Matt 17:5).

Listen to him. A simple command concerning a powerful message. A supremely lived life as a lesson; a supreme lesson for life. Listen. Listen to him—not just what he said; listen to his life itself. No one before or after has ever spoken and lived as Jesus did (John 7:46). No one could claim to control the origin and destiny of the world as he did. No one was ever able to do the things he did. The "super" was indeed "natural" to him: walking on water, commanding the winds and the waves, giving sight to the blind, feeding the hungry, healing the lame, giving life to the dead, and even himself being brutally executed and resurrected before ascending back into heaven before the still-shaken apostles.

No one ever spoke like he did. "You will do well to pay attention to it, as to a light shining in a dark place, until the day dawns and the morning star rises in your hearts" (2 Pet 1:19). Pay attention. Listen to him and watch the day dawn and the morning star rise in your heart. Light—warmth, security, enlightenment.

Following a Jew killed some two thousand years ago makes no sense from a merely human perspective. However, if the Bible is true, he is not really dead; he is risen! He showed himself alive with many "convincing proofs" (Acts 1:3). His message is as "living and active" today as it ever was (Heb 4:12). His words are life.

He is in fact the "author and perfecter of our faith" (Heb 12:2)—the trailblazer. Focus on him and follow (Heb 3:1). And experience the goodness of God (Heb 1:3).

Jesus, after his baptism, went about to show us how to win at life—how to truly live. In doing so, the Holy Spirit led him to take Satan on immediately.

Then he climbed the mountain of God to teach us how to do the same as he did. He invites you to come up on the mountain with him, so to speak, to be with him and to learn from him.

Reflections:
1. Something to ask yourself: What do I really believe about Jesus?
2. Something to think about: Where did my beliefs come from, and why do I still believe them?
3. Something to believe: Truth is often more difficult to discover and believe than what is false.
4. Something to pray: Father, please help me to have an honest heart, and please reveal pure truth to me.
5. Something to memorize: "I am the way and the truth and the life. No one comes to the father except through me" (Jesus, in John 14:6).
6. Something to do: Make a commitment to spend time daily seeking truth. Or are you perhaps too afraid the truth might disturb what you already believe?

2

The Challenge

(Matt 4:1–11)

*Then Jesus was led by the Spirit into the desert to be tempted
by the devil. After fasting forty days and forty nights, he
was hungry. The tempter came to him and said, "If you are
the Son of God, tell these stones to become bread."
Jesus answered, "It is written: 'Man does not live on bread alone,
but on every word that comes from the mouth of God.'"
Then the devil took him to the holy city and had him stand
on the highest point of the temple. "If you are the Son of
God," he said, "throw yourself down. For it is written:
'He will command his angels concerning you, and they will lift you up
in their hands, so that you will not strike your foot against a stone.'"
Jesus answered him, "It is also written:
'Do not put the Lord your God to the test.'"
Again, the devil took him to a very high mountain and showed him
all the kingdoms of the world and their splendor. "All this I will
give you," he said, "if you will bow down and worship me."
Jesus said to him, "Away from me, Satan! For it is writ-
ten: 'Worship the Lord your God, and serve him only.'"
Then the devil left him, and angels came and attended him.*

After our initiation into the kingdom, Satan too will challenge
us as he did Jesus. The Spirit allows us to be tested as he allowed

Jesus to be. However, he always provides a way of deliverance (1 Cor 10:13).

There were three great temptations Jesus had to face in the wilderness: the temptation *to prove himself*, the temptation *to prove God*, and the temptation *to personally possess power*. Three P's of spiritual warfare. Don't forget them, because Satan is very repetitive in his temptations. You do not need to prove yourself. As Christians, we are validated by our salvation through Christ and his work in us, especially our weaknesses. We were clearly shown to be priceless to God when he did what he did in sacrificing Christ for us. Most importantly, you do not need to prove God to anyone, including Satan. We must not put God to the test. He will not be studied as a human test case. He will not allow himself to be put in a test tube or be observed under a microscope. Further, you do not need to truly possess anything; neither do you need power. Christ taught us to lead from the bottom, not from the top. We serve a "meek and lowly" God, not a "high and mighty" one. When we commit our lives to Christ, we give him everything we own and everything we are. He will entrust us with the things that are best for us. Anything acquired through evil means, even those that may seem good, will prove most deadly, unless of course they are later consecrated by God through your repentance. You will most assuredly experience such testing in your own life.

Satan challenged Jesus in the wilderness just as he challenged Eve and Adam in the Garden: "If you are the Son of God, throw yourself down. For it is written 'He will command his angels concerning you and they will lift you up.'" Again, to an obviously very hungry Jesus, "Tell these stones to become bread." Concerning all the early kingdoms, Satan said to Jesus, "All this I will give you if you will bow down and worship me."

Prove you are the Son of God. Prove God will take care of you. Possess it all—own lands and kingdoms.

In our Christian walks, Satan will use these three temptations over and over again with us, and we must master them. Our testimony to ourselves—to our righteousness, to our sincerity, to our commitment—means nothing. Only God's testimony is true.

We do not need to prove God to anyone. "The fool says in his heart, 'There is no God'" (Ps 14:1). Frankly, we do not even need to prove ourselves to any other human either, including ourselves. "I do not even judge myself" (1 Cor 4:3–4). There's only one vote that matters, and that vote is God's. "If God is for us, who can be against us?" (Rom 8: 31). Whether God leads us through a valley or onto a mountaintop, God will sustain us. The angels will attend us when God is ready—when Satan is not around.

You do not need to worship anyone or anything but God. Through Christ, you already possess the world. You are an heir to all of God's riches. Satan and the world can give you nothing. Well, nothing but a curse.

Be prepared for your test. It has already come if you are a Christian, and it will surely come again.

Reflections:
1. Something to ask yourself: What has been my greatest spiritual test up to this point in my life?
2. Something to think about: Why does God allow us to be tested by Satan?
3. Something to believe: The tests of life are not designed to destroy us but to strengthen us.
4. Something to pray: Lord, help me to recognize Satan's testing and to face it with the wisdom of Christ.
5. Something to memorize: "Then the devil left him" (Matt 4:11).
6. Something to do: Reread Matt 4:1–10 and compare Jesus's tests to one or some of your own.

3

Possessed

(Matt 4:12–17)

When Jesus heard that John had been put in prison, he returned to Galilee. Leaving Nazareth, he went and lived in Capernaum, which was by the lake in the area of Zebulun and Naphtali—to fulfill what was said through the prophet Isaiah: "Land of Zebulun and land of Naphtali, the way to the sea, along the Jordan, Galilee of the Gentiles— the people living in darkness have seen a great light; on those living in the land of the shadow of death a light has dawned." From that time on Jesus began to preach, "Repent, for the kingdom of heaven is near."

The world around us is like a raging river. It wants us to flow with it, to go where it goes, and to end up where it ends up. The Bible tells us not to do that. It tells us we must not conform to the world—not go with it (Rom 12:2). God wants us to go with him and to let him lead us instead. He wants to be our king. He wants us to be part of his kingdom. To do that, we must be pressed into his mold, not the world's. We must flow with him and his kingdom, not with the world. We must make Jesus our lord and king. "Repent, for the kingdom of heaven is near." Jesus preached it then. He's still preaching it.

As then, so it is now, at any given time: some are in the kingdom of God, others are near the kingdom of God, and far too many are far from the kingdom of God. Being in Jesus's kingdom is not simply about "being Christian" by religion or even attending church. It is not at all about being religious! Following Jesus is about having faith that he is truly the king. If he is, then we will genuinely want to follow him, let him be our lord, and take our instructions from him.

To follow Jesus is to be a disciple of Jesus. Discipleship is about being owned by Christ. Discipleship is followship. Discipleship is also about passionately owning Christ personally as our leader. When we are close to making a decision to do that, the kingdom is near. When we actually do it, we are in the kingdom. That is still the only choice Jesus gives. Any other choice comes from someone other than him.

"A light has dawned." For some, however, there is no light. Darkness prevails with them because God does not rule their lives. The Christian has chosen to accept the gift of God. Light—a great light. The disciple of Christ has chosen not to live in the land of the shadow of death. Christ leads us from it. The Christian has chosen light. Christians have chosen to live on the mountaintop with God.

The choice is not about being a church member; neither is it about living better. The choice is not about being good or learning about God. The choice is God. Repentance—changing your mind completely.

"Repent, for the kingdom of heaven is near." Jesus's own words. Isaiah said, "Seek the Lord while he may be found; call on him while he is near" (Isa 55:6). The kingdom is not always near; God may not always be found.

You have found him or have a chance to find him. Seek him. Repent. In your heart of hearts, turn away from the world—from being possessed by it. Turn to God, to be possessed by him.

At times, each of us will be tempted to undo our repentance, to "unchange" our minds, so to speak, and to turn back to the world—to "unrepent." It is said of the children of Israel that, after all they had been through in Egypt and after God had delivered them from it, that they "in their hearts turned back to

Egypt" (Acts 7:39). Do not for one second entertain the thought of turning back (2 Pet 2:20–21). Make the choice once and for all for God. Choose God. At work, at home, when you're alone, when you play, when you sleep. Choose God.

"Repent, for the kingdom of heaven is near."

Reflections:

1. Something to ask yourself: Am I only under the influence of God, or under his control?
2. Something to think about: What does it look like to be in God's kingdom?
3. Something to believe: God is able to deliver on his kingdom promise.
4. Something to pray: God, draw me near to the kingdom as you draw it near to me.
5. Something to memorize: "Seek the Lord while he may be found; call on him while he is near" (Isa 55:6).
6. Something to do: Review all the things that you own, do, and love, considering which of these might be owning you.

4

Who Is Doing All the Work Here?

(Matt 4:18–22)

As Jesus was walking beside the Sea of Galilee, he saw two broth-ers, Simon called Peter and his brother Andrew. They were casting a net into the lake, for they were fishermen. "Come, follow me," Jesus said, "and I will make you fishers of men." At once they left their nets and followed him. Going on from there, he saw two other broth-ers, James son of Zebedee and his brother John. They were in a boat with their father Zebedee, preparing their nets. Jesus called them, and immediately they left the boat and their father and followed him.

"I will make you," Jesus says. The greatest challenge of disciple-ship is to let Jesus lead and do his work in us. "We are his work-manship," not our own (Eph 2:10). When Jesus possesses you, you become the work of Christ. So let Jesus do the work!

You may believe that you choose God and that you choose to do right and that you choose to serve Him. Wrong. Well, mostly wrong. "You did not choose me, but I chose you" (John 15:16). God's election is a great mystery. "Many are invited but few are chosen" (Matt 22:14). "No one can come to me unless my Father who sent me draws him" (John 6:44). But if you have been drawn to him, you can be chosen.

As a Christian, you have been chosen. You are to be his work, not your own. He possesses you. "God works in you to will and to act according to his good purpose" (Phil 2:13).

Your goal every day must be to surrender to Christ. He will give you the will to act according to his good purposes. Focus on him. Follow him. Let nothing deter you from this task. Trust and obey.

When his will is being accomplished in you, you will experience your purpose. Many others will be called through you. If you feel the call to reach out to another, be sure to do so. Just make the call. If you are called to help another, do so. If you feel urged to serve in any way, do it. Act. It is your calling to do it. It is God's way of working on you, in you, and through you.

Christ will lead you to help him fish for men—to help and to lead and to serve others. Yield to his work in you. And go fishing.

Reflections:
1. Something to ask: What is my role to be in reaching out to others?
2. Something to think about: All the correlations that exist between fishing for fish and fishing for people.
3. Something to believe: That God has called you. You could not even seek to follow him if he has not done this.
4. Something to pray: God, help me to not only know about the calling, help me to come to know *my* calling.
5. Something to memorize: "You did not choose me, but I chose you" (John 15:16).
6. Something to do: Call someone today whom you have not talked to in a while. Ask the person how she or he is doing. Ask how she or he is *really* doing. Then listen. The Spirit will lead you in what else to do, if anything.

5

Good News

(Matt 4:23-25)

Jesus went throughout Galilee, teaching in their synagogues, preaching the good news of the kingdom, and healing every disease and sickness among the people. News about him spread all over Syria, and people brought to him all who were ill with various diseases, those suffering severe pain, the demon-possessed, those having seizures, and the paralyzed, and he healed them. Large crowds from Galilee, the Decapolis, Jerusalem, Judea and the region across the Jordan followed him.

Jesus preached the good news of the kingdom. Good news. We all want to hear it so much, but too often we hear so little of it in this world. In fact, through the modern media, we are constantly bombarded with the bad news. Makes it sound like Satan is winning, doesn't it? What percentage of the news that you hear on a daily basis is bad, and how much is good? I think you get the point.

But, Jesus did not just preach the good news; he *was* good news. Notice what the scripture says he did: "...healing every disease and sickness among the people...he healed them." Luke simply tells us, "He went around doing good and healing all who were under the power of the devil, because God was with him" (Acts 10:38). That got the attention of large crowds. It was good news lived out.

Francis of Assisi said something like, "Preach the gospel (good news) wherever you go, and if necessary use words." Jesus apparently *spoke* relatively few words. He *was* the word, though. His actions were his word. "If every one of them [the things he did] were written down, I suppose that even the whole world would not have room for the books that would be written" (John 21:25).

"Do not merely listen to the word and so deceive yourselves. Do what it says" (James 1:22). Faith is *active*. Do not be led astray to believe that faith is something that is inside of you only. Faith is your life. Your faith is seen in your life. "Faith by itself, if it is not accompanied by action, is dead" (James 2:17). Your faith is not defined by what you say or what you feel; faith is seen in how you live. *Be* good news. You can indeed have works without faith, but by the Bible's own definition, you cannot have faith without action!

The good news is about healing. It is about seeing the pain removed. It is about helping and caring and sharing. It is about telling others the truth—that God loves them not because of *what* they are, but because of *who* they are—his image-bearers. And who God is—their loving, beckoning Father! It is about telling them that God chooses them and that he wants them. Yes, God seeks us out. And he wants us to reach out to him (Acts 17:27). And that he gave his *best* for them when they were at *their worst* (Rom 5:6–8).

Let him make your life good news too.

Reflections:
1. Something to ask: What percentage of the news that I hear daily is bad, and how much is good?
2. Something to think about: How much good news do you live out to others each day?
3. Something to believe: It is really not that hard to be many individuals' best friends, as so many people do not really have any truly good friends.

4. Something to pray: Lord, make me the good news of Christ to those all around me.

5. Something to memorize: "He went around doing good and healing all who were under the power of the devil, because God was with him" (Acts 10:38).

6. Something to do: Go do something extravagantly nice today for someone who desperately needs good news. Be too generous.

6

Up on the Mountain with God

(Matt 5:1-2)

Now when he saw the crowds, he went up on a mountainside and sat down. His disciples came to him, and he began to teach them, saying...

"The crowds were amazed at his teaching, because he taught as one who had authority, and not as their teachers of the law" (Matt 7:28–29). By the time Jesus set foot on the earth, the Jews had developed a deeply entrenched oral tradition that had originated with the Law of Moses but had diverged from it significantly over the years. It had developed over the centuries through the teachings of the religious leaders and rabbis. Jesus said it even nullified God's word (Matt 15:1–9).

Jesus does not teach as a man, though. This was (and is still) apparent. He teaches as God, because he is God (John 1:1). "He spoke as one who had authority and not as their teachers of the law" (Matt 7:29). They were on the mountain with God. His words were not, are not, just expressions; they are life (Deut 32:47). His words are not meandering thoughts and reflections of just another man; they are the revelation of God himself. Jesus told them who God was. He showed them they could be like him. He told them what God was like by his life and by his teaching.

"Man does not live on bread alone, but on every word that comes from the mouth of God" (Matt 4:4). Jesus's words are the food that gives you life—spiritual life. Real life. Eat so that you may live. Jesus's "flesh is real food" and his "blood is real drink" (John 6:55). Jesus said to a Samaritan woman: "If you knew the gift of God and who it is that asks you for a drink, you would have asked him and he would have given you living water" (John 4:10).

Eat so others may live too. "Let the word of Christ dwell in you richly as you teach and admonish one another with all wisdom" (Col 3:16).

Other words you speak may pacify, but they will not satisfy. They cannot really. Other words you speak may sympathize, but they cannot sanctify. Only the words of Christ give life.

Paul learned the lesson of Jesus well: "I resolved to know nothing…except Jesus Christ and him crucified" (1 Cor 2:2). Resolve now to fill yourself with the words that give life. Know him.

Reflections:
1. Something to ask: Am I tuned in to the words of Jesus, truly tuned in only to him?
2. Something to think about: How do ingesting and digesting the words of Christ and enjoying their life-giving nourishment correlate with our physically eating, digesting, and being nourished?
3. Something to believe: Jesus is always speaking through his Word, his Spirit, and his Creation.
4. Something to pray: Jesus, help me to hear your voice and your teaching.
5. Something to memorize: "Man does not live on bread alone, but on every word that comes from the mouth of God" (Matt 4:4).
6. Something to do: Read the entire Sermon on the Mount (Matt 5–7) aloud as though you are sitting at Jesus's very feet. Or have someone else read it to you. Picture him there speaking the words.

7

Go for Broke

(Matt 5:3)

Blessed are the poor in spirit, for theirs is the kingdom of heaven.

Being broke is not fun. Not in a worldly sense, anyway. I have been broke. In college, I rolled my pennies to do my laundry. I have borrowed money to eat. Poor—not a favorite word around town. This is not a popular subject.

Poor people are poor because of flaws, because of mistakes, because of misfortune or insanity. Right? No sane person chooses to be poor. Right? Well, not all the time. Sometimes poverty is the right choice. The wise choice.

In fact, the Christian has chosen to be poor. When you choose Jesus, you choose poverty—to own nothing. "If you want to be perfect, go, sell your possessions and give to the poor, and you will have treasure in heaven. Then come, follow me" (Matt 19:21). And, in this poverty, God possesses you—"theirs [yours] is the kingdom of heaven." He wants only you. Nothing else is necessary. You are not to bring anything to God except you. You seek him first, and he will provide you what you need (Matt 6:33). And he will also take away what you do not need (John 15:1–2). Simply put: "Present your bodies as living sacrifices to God" (Rom 12:1). Your body then becomes God's house—his temple (1 Cor 6:19–20).

As a citizen of the kingdom of heaven, God does not allow you to actually possess anything in this world. "Any of you who does not give up everything he has cannot be my disciple" (Luke 14:33). You only use the earthly possessions for a short while, anyway. They stay when you go home—your house, your clothes, your loved ones. They belong to God. You are the trustee of what God now owns—you. And as a trustee, you must be faithful to manage God's possessions in a trustworthy manner (1 Cor 4:2).

But you? God lets you choose your destiny, at least in a way. You have to give you to God, though. Although he can, he will not take you by force. He calls you by invitation. He wants you to be full of him and not full of yourself.

"Whoever finds his life will lose it" (Luke 9:24). If you seek to possess your possessions, then your possessions will possess you. "Do not store up for yourself treasures on earth…For where your treasure is, there your heart will be also" (Matt 6:19).

You have to give up the claim to that over which God has given you power—you and anything the world might say is yours. "Poor in spirit." It is only when you give up claim to yourself that God will possess you—can possess you. Then the kingdom of heaven and all its "riches" becomes yours (Eph 1:17–19). Instead of making your life about earthly riches, "go for broke" in Christ. Become beyond rich.

Reflections:
1. Something to ask: What (or who) in this world can lay claim to owning any part of me?
2. Something to think about: How much of your life is really all about you, and how much of your life is really about God and others?
3. Something to believe: If you truly lose your life for God, you will truly find the incredible life Jesus promises.
4. Something to pray: Lord, lead me to be empty of myself—poor in spirit—as you emptied yourself for me (Phil 2:5–8).

5. Something to memorize: "Any of you who does not give up everything he has cannot be my disciple" (Luke 14:33).

6. Something to do: Give up or give away something that is "possessing" you. Pray for God to reveal what it is. Pray to God about where or to whom to give it.

8

Celebrate Sadness

(Matt 5:4)

Blessed are those who mourn, for they will be comforted.

We mourn in secret. We mostly hide to mourn—"I don't want anybody to see me crying." As if any normal person does. "I hate to cry." Profound words, huh? Who enjoys crying or seeks to cry? Mourning is a bad thing in our earthly way of thinking. We do not like to mourn. We certainly do not like to celebrate being sad. But "blessed are those who mourn."

I heard a psychologist on the radio say one time that, when loved ones die, if we do not mourn for them, then every time we think of them, we will mourn again inwardly for the rest of our lives. I believe that. And it is generally true about anything, in fact, that has seriously hurt us in some way.

If we are to experience the blessedness of Christ, then we must mourn for the old self, which has been put to death, lest we mourn again every time we remember our former lives. We will not have blessedness if our memory betrays us to the perpetual sadness of an "unmourned" past.

But, if we truly mourn for the tragedy that is the old self, then we are open to the future comforts God will bring in the kingdom. Comforts that only those with the Spirit can accept. "The man without the Spirit does not accept the things that come from the Spirit of God" (1 Cor 2:14).

Go ahead; mourn. "Grieve mourn and wail. Change your laughter to mourning and your joy to gloom." Let God give you his comfort, and true joy will come your way (2 Cor 1:3–5).

"Every word of God is flawless" (Prov 30:5). "Do not rely on your own insight" (Prov 3:5). If you are predisposed to thinking that mourning can lead to nothing good, then you are doomed to a life of mourning—but the wrong kind. If you will trust God that on the other side of this mourning one finds true comfort, then God's utter bliss awaits you. You are ready to live atop God's mountain.

There was nothing good in your past life. It was completely toxic and contaminated. It was simply a devastated war zone. There is nothing you should bring with you. Your sins do not make you more useful to God; rather, they make you useless to God. Nothing good comes from sin. All good comes from God. God will use you—the person you are right now—to advance his cause. No matter where you have been or what you have done, he will make it work out for good (Rom 8:28). He will make it work out in accordance with his purpose (Eph 1:11). But do not for one minute think your sinful self has any use in the kingdom.

Leave the old self behind—completely. Have a funeral in your heart. Gaze on the corrupted mortal self that lies wounded unto death. Weep, mourn, and wail over what you have been— what you have done to God, others, and yourself. Then and only then will the God of heaven bring you the comfort you have so desperately sought but were unable to find. "Whoever loses his life for me will save it" (Luke 9:24). A serendipity, I believe.

Reflections:

1. Something to ask yourself: Am I so caught up in being happy that I fail to be the mourner God so desires me to be?

2. Something to think about: Do I trust God enough to believe that mourning as he mourns will bring utter joy as God himself experiences it?

3. Something to believe: The rainbow of God's bliss is deeply embedded in his clouds of mourning.

4. Something to pray: God, help me to be brave enough to wade into the sadness of this cursed world, rather than to seek its temporary consolations.

5. Something to memorize: "Blessed are those who mourn, for they will be comforted" (Matt 5:4).

6. Something to do: Make a list of a few people around you that are suffering because of poor or nonexistent relationships with God. In a humble, godly way, mourn in prayer for them.

9

You Can Own It All

(Matt 5:5)

Blessed are the meek, for they will inherit the earth.

Meek equals timid, mousy, and shy, right? Wrong. At least, it is wrong the way God sees it. Meekness is humility. To be humble does not constitute weakness. In fact, to be humble is to recognize one's strength and not flaunt or misuse it.

Meekness is power under control. To be meek is to know what we are capable of doing, but not having to do it unless it is the right thing to do. Then we certainly can and will do it.

Meek is a powerful stallion, harnessed for his master's use. Meekness is a powerful engine at the disposal of the driver. Meekness is a raging river directed through electrical turbines to light a city.

Meekness is not weakness. True meekness is powerful. Meekness is submission. Jesus was meek. Remember? Meekness, rather, is the power of God channeled through your mortal body to do the will and work of God. "Laboring with all his energy, which so powerfully works in me" (Col 1:29).

Jesus said he, and thus God, was "gentle and humble" (Matt 11:29). Jesus was indeed meek, but he certainly was not weak! And he does not intend for us to be weak. Just meek.

Meekness is not passiveness, even though it is humble. Rather, it is the harnessing of every ounce of one's God-given power to do God's bidding: "Yet not as I will, but as you will" (Matt 26:39). It is the carrying out of the divine will. Our missions are "sub" (under) his mission. Submission.

Meekness is power, because it is in sync with the ultimate power of the universe—God. "They [you] will inherit the earth." What Satan offered Jesus ("All this I will give you" [Matt 4:9]), God actually does give us. In Christ, ours are "the riches of his glorious inheritance in the saints" (Eph 1:18). You will possess all that is God's.

Let God harness you, a consecrated vessel of the Holy Spirit, and you will see his power at work in you. "He [you] will do even greater things than these" (what Christ had been doing; John 14:12).

Yield your will to his as he did his to God's (John 14:31). Yield your control to him. Submit. When you do, you really can have it all—you will "inherit the earth." God's way. Not by the sword and not with money, as humans do. You will inherit the earth the right way.

Reflections:
1. Something to ask yourself: Why must I be meek in order for God to harness and empower me?
2. Something to think about: Are you meek, or are you simply timid or weak?
3. Something to believe: God can do infinitely more through even our weaknesses than we can do through all our supposed strengths apart from him.
4. Something to pray: Father, reveal in me my hard, unmalleable parts, and give me a heart of surrender that you may mold and harness every part of me.
5. Something to memorize: "Blessed are the meek, for they will inherit the earth" (Matt 5:5).
6. Something to do: Ask a spiritual friend or advisor what part of you that they think might be the hardest for God to mold.

10

Start the Day on an Empty Stomach

(Matt 5:6)

Blessed are those who hunger and thirst for righteousness, for they will be filled.

Have you ever been really hungry? Of course you have. Have you ever almost starved to death? (Doubtful, for most who read this.)

Have you ever been so thirsty that you almost died of thirst? "No, not really," you say. Well, in a way, you actually have; you just did not know the symptoms. Spiritually, it is as with our physical bodies: by the time we feel thirsty, we are already dehydrating.

Remember the time you were so down that you did not want to go on? Remember the time you lost the loved one and you hurt so badly, you wanted to give up? Remember the time you were so lonely, you felt like quitting? You were hungry and thirsty to the point of not being able to continue. But you did not recognize the spiritual signals and hunger pangs.

One problem is that, as with very small children and physical needs, we do not know how to interpret our spiritual hunger and thirst. Another problem is that when we recognize we are hungry and thirsty, we often attempt to satisfy our craving through what is not real food or drink. We seek out pleasure, adventure, or relationships. We go out to eat, we overeat, we go to a movie, or we attend some entertainment event. We go shopping, gamble, take a vacation, or buy a new car. We read a self-help book, go to a counselor, talk to a friend, or go to bed. We get cosmetic surgery, start a new diet, or train for and run a marathon. We try yoga, learn about some Eastern religion, or start attending a church nearby. And so on and so on. Many of those things are OK; many are good within the right context. However, some are just bad for us. And none will do any good unless the act is imbued with God's Spirit, his wisdom, and his power. "Why spend money on what is not bread and your labor on what does not satisfy" (Isa 55:2)?

The world tells us satisfaction will come around a campfire with the right people and the right alcoholic beverage. Or with the "right" person—often preferably a new "right" person in a relationship saturated with infatuation and allure. Or by driving a certain beautiful, powerful, and trendy new car on a mountain's hairpin curve. Really?

The world would have us believe we will find satisfaction in looks and money, and in comforts and physical pleasures. The world tells us that "gusto" comes from worldly pleasure and that we need to grab for it.

The world is very, very wrong. Just observe it. As modern cultures have accumulated wealth and possessions, and as humanity has enjoyed pleasures and conveniences unknown in previous generations, rates of depression, stress, suicide, broken homes, crimes of all kinds, and so on have only sky-rocketed. Because none of these pleasures within themselves are real drink. None of them are real bread. In fact, compared to the real thing, all of it is junk food that only sours our appetites for real food and real drink. So not only are we not starving for good food and drink, we are turned off by it. We are already full!

God says our hunger and thirst will be satisfied only by the reality of the cross: we are loved beyond imagination and wanted beyond comprehension; we are priceless at our worst; and we have been offered the very essence of God to be in us. Jesus's flesh and blood are to be our food and drink (John 6:55). Real sustenance. "Real food" and "real drink."

"Righteousness, righteousness is what I long for. Righteousness is what I need," the song pines. Hunger and thirst for the righteous, God's righteousness, and you will be filled. "God made him who had no sin to be sin for us, so that in him we might become the righteousness of God" (2 Cor 5:21). You will not become righteous before God by being good. God will see you as righteous when you come to trust that *he* is righteous. He wants you to trust him, not yourself or others. To believe. In him and his goodness, not your own. To walk by faith in Christ.

"He condemned sin...in order that the righteous requirements of the law might be fully met in us" (Rom 8:3–4). He basically "took out" what was capable of "taking us out."

Quench your thirst and satisfy your hunger by the "righteousness that comes from God and is by faith" (Phil 3:9). Get to know him better and better. Believe him. Trust him. Hunger and thirst for him. Then and only then will you be filled.

Do not live on an empty stomach. Do not try to run on an empty tank. Everything the world so slavishly seeks in sinful and worldly ways, but is never satisfied with, is found in a true relationship with Christ. He is beautiful beyond description, his love is limitless, his power is boundless, his grace is incomprehensible, and his patience is immeasurable. Feed yourselves on these realities.

Reflections:
1. Something to ask: What are my own spiritual and emotional hunger pangs that I might be likely to ignore?
2. Something to think about: What have you spent so much of your life and effort seeking that has not brought true satisfaction?
3. Something to believe: Jesus is the answer to every question, the solution to every problem, and the balm for every ill.

4. Something to pray: Lord, help me find the secret to everlasting contentment found only in Christ (Phil 4:4–13).

5. Something to memorize: "Blessed are those who hunger and thirst for righteousness, for they will be filled" (Matt 5:6).

6. Something to do: Listen for spiritual hunger pangs—signs of discontent, fear, anxiety, lack of feeling fulfilled, etc. Ponder how Christ has taught us to meet our needs with "real food."

11

Throw Away Your Yardstick

(Matt 5:7)

Blessed are the merciful, for they will be shown mercy.

"With the measure you use, it will be measured to you" (Matt 7:2). Are you a merciful person? Or are you harsh and cynical toward others' weaknesses? Do you enjoy seeing the punishment and pain of others when you feel they "deserve" it? Then you must conform to the will of Christ, or you will experience harshness and cynicism yourself.

"Neither do I condemn you. Go now and leave your life of sin" (John 8:11). Is there someone you are condemning just now? Is there someone of whom you are constantly critical? Your husband? Your wife? Your parents? Your children? Your church or its leaders? A friend? The government or a political party? Is there a sin in others that makes you feel particularly harsh toward them, or somehow better than they are? If so, then how you view and treat them is how you must expect others to view and treat you.

"He is patient with you, not wanting anyone to perish, but everyone to come to repentance" (2 Pet 3:9). In your life, do you manifest the desire to see everyone change? Then accept them as they are. "Accept one another, then, just as Christ accepted you, in order to bring praise to God" (Rom 15:7). Accept them as they are and free them to change. Accept yourself so that you will be free to change.

God is not praised through our self-righteous criticism and condemnation of others. Rather, he is praised through the crucifixion of our own self-centered approaches and our surrender to his will and attitude toward them. He saved us so he could demonstrate his incredible mercy to the world through us (Eph 2:6–7)!

"He had compassion on them, because they were harassed and helpless, like sheep without a shepherd" (Matt 9:36). Jesus had compassion on others. Change your view of others—"So from now on we regard no one from a worldly point of view. Though we once regarded Christ in this way, we do so no longer" (2 Cor 5:16). Have compassion for others. And for yourself, for goodness' sake!

You must learn to look at others through the lens of the Christ on the cross. God does. Throw away your yardstick. It is not accurate anyway. It's not helpful. Yardsticks ultimately become sticks to beat with rather than boards to build with.

Then you will be shown mercy.

Reflections:
1. Something to ask yourself: What measuring stick do I use to judge others?
2. Something to think about: Whom might you actually help by being a fan rather than a critic?
3. Something to believe: We always perform better in front of our fans than we do our critics.
4. Something to pray: Lord, help me see others through the merciful and compassionate eyes of Christ.
5. Something to memorize: "Blessed are the merciful, for they will be shown mercy" (Matt 5:7).
6. Something to do: Make a list of those whom you feel most critical toward. Consider the measuring stick you are using to be critical of them. Picture yourself breaking that stick and throwing it away. Now picture yourself measuring people with the yardstick of the cross, so to speak.

12

The One Thing

(Matt 5:8)

Blessed are the pure in heart, for they will see God.

"They will see God." Only unimpeded by the haze of worldliness, can we see God. Unpolluted by the world's corruption, we can see only God. Creation itself declares God—it shouts in proclamation his name and wonder. Unclouded by worldliness, we see the one thing. And only unclouded from the haze of worldliness can we see God.

What impurities do you have in your life that obscure God from you? What worldly relics from the past have you possessed and sought to bring with you into God's kingdom? When Achan stole items that had been devoted to the Lord and buried them under his tent, he was under a curse. Joshua said to him, "The Lord will bring disaster on you today" (Josh 7:25). Do you perhaps have things hidden in your life that you are not supposed to have? Have you unwittingly tried to consecrate to God that which is accursed?

"Since, then, you have been raised with Christ, set your hearts on things above" (Col 3:1). What do you have your affections set on? "Rather, clothe yourselves with the Lord Jesus Christ, and do not think about how to gratify the desires of the sinful nature" (Rom 13:14). Is it your house? Is it your car? Is it your hobby or recreation? Is it your family? "Anyone who loves his father or mother more than me is not worthy of me" (Matt 10:27).

Only when your view of God through the cross of Christ is unobstructed by other affections can you truly see God. Only when the cross becomes your unobstructed focus can you rightly see God. Only when nothing stands between you and God except the cross can you see only God.

If you have preserved affections that have not been consecrated for God and are not qualified for consecration, you face disaster. Affections that stand between you and God are idols—"You shall have no other gods before me" (Exod 20:3). You must lay these before the cross and offer them to God for his possession and for his destruction. If he chooses, you will find them again in your life, and in the right proportion and priority. If he does not, you will not be giving them up; you will getting rid of them.

God *is* the one thing.

Reflections:

1. Something to ask: What affections might be contaminating my purity before God?
2. Something to think about: The only things that really matter today are those that will still matter in a thousand years and on into eternity.
3. Something to believe: All that stands between God and me becomes worthless when God becomes to me priceless.
4. Something to pray: Father, give me a pure heart—a heart that is only about one thing—you.
5. Something to memorize: "Blessed are the pure in heart, for they will see God" (Matt 5:8).
6. Something to do: Make a list of the people and things you most love, the things you spend your money on, and the things and people you spend your time on. Consider which of those you may consistently put before God, or around which you consistently arrange your walk with God. Reprioritize accordingly.

13

Peacemaking

(Matt 5:9)

Blessed are the peacemakers, for they will be called sons of God.

"Do not suppose that I have come to bring peace to the earth, I did not come to bring peace, but a sword" (Matt 10:34). Jesus confuses us sometimes, doesn't he? At least until he explains himself. And then, still, sometimes…

Make no mistake—there is no peace between light and darkness. "What fellowship can light have with darkness" (2 Cor 6:14)? One who is not surrendered to God cannot accept the things of God, as they ultimately will seem so foolish in his way of thinking (1 Cor 2:14). Whoever is not for Christ is against him (Matt 12:30).

Do not expect your friends from the world to understand your "otherworldliness." They cannot. They cannot understand, and they cannot accept it. Do not try to make peace with anyone outside of Christ. Not that kind of peace. You simply cannot. However, as far as it lies within you, be in a peaceful relationship with everyone (Rom 12:18). Sometimes, though, it simply is not up to you. Real peace at the deepest level cannot be achieved with one who is not in Christ. That is the same as trying to bring God and Satan to the negotiating table to agree on anything.

It just will not happen—"What agreement is there between the temple of God and idols?" (2 Cor 6:16).

At its core, peacemaking is about bringing others to peace with God. Many are unwittingly at odds with him. Others became so by decision. God wants us to do something about it. He wants us to be peacemakers. "God was reconciling the world to himself in Christ, not counting men's sins against them. And he has committed to us the message of reconciliation. We are therefore Christ's ambassadors, as though God were making his appeal through us" (2 Cor 5:20).

God will not send you on an impossible mission. Rather, God sends you on a possible mission—that of reconciling honest, truth-seeking men and women to God. He has made provision, through the cross, for it to happen for every person. He arms you with the peace treaty called the gospel. And yours is simply to plant the seed of the gospel and water it as you can. You do not have to make it grow. You cannot do that. That is what God does to his seed in fertile hearts (1 Cor 3:7; Matt 13:23).

True peace is found only in Jesus, the "bond of peace," the superglue of the spiritual realm. "For he himself is our peace, who has made the two one and has destroyed the barrier, the dividing wall of hostility" (Eph 2:14). Peace with God is found at the cross—through Jesus Christ. In fact, he is the only way to God (John 14:6). The lines between God and Satan are clearly drawn. God's judgment on Satan is final—outer darkness, eternal banishment. Jesus saw Satan thrown out of heaven (Luke 10:18).

The Son himself made bringing peace between God and mankind his mission: "For the Son of Man came to seek and to save what was lost" (Luke 19:10). God seeks sincere, seeking people to worship him (John 4:23). He is indeed the "Prince of Peace" (Isa 9:6).

If you will yield yourself as an ambassador of God and a fisher of men, bringing people to peace with God through the gospel of the cross, you will identify most fully with the Son. You will, in fact, be called a "son [child] of God."

Make his mission of peace your mission of peace. The proclamation and ministry of the gospel of Christ, evangelism, is the core of peacemaking. Building up other disciples is strengthening and maintaining that peace. Real peace only exists in God's kingdom though.

Be a peacemaker—a real child of God! Creation is waiting for you to reveal yourself too (Rom 8:19).

Reflections:
1. Something to ask: What does real peace even look like?
2. Something to think about: Is the "peace" I experience with those outside of Christ the right kind, and is the peace I experience with other Christians real peace?
3. Something to believe: Eternal peace can only be found in Christ.
4. Something to pray: God, make me a peacemaker the way Jesus was a peacemaker.
5. Something to memorize: "Blessed are the peacemakers, for they will be called sons of God" (Matt 5:9).
6. Something to do: Pray for someone whom you know is not at total peace with God. Do one other thing to try to help her or him come closer to God.

14

Be Prepared; Be Unafraid

(Matt 5:10–12)

Blessed are those who are persecuted because of righteousness, for theirs is the kingdom of heaven. Blessed are you when people insult you, persecute you and falsely say all kinds of evil against you because of me. Rejoice and be glad, because great is your reward in heaven, for in the same way they persecuted the prophets who were before you.

"Leave." The gruff, angry voice spewed venom over the phone. Dial tone. My wife hung up, bewildered. She was home alone with the kids. She became a little shaken and unsettled. Afraid.

Later, "Leave." It was I this time who answered. The voice sounded evil, menacing. It clearly reminded me of a voice in an earlier time of my ministry that said to me: "You have forsaken us (unbelievers), and I'm going to destroy you!" A bizarre, shaggy-headed fellow I had reached out to briefly had said it to me. But I was again taken aback and failed immediately to recognize who it was who was really speaking. I was shaken for sure after both incidents.

This was before cell phones and caller ID; tracking calls was much more difficult. And if you did, and if and when someone was caught making threatening calls, you had no choice whether to prosecute, as the phone company retained that right itself. We declined to do that because we felt certain it was someone from the new church we were leading, and we did not want to have a church member placed in the hands of law enforcement. The calls stopped as quickly as they had started. It was not a really big deal, but it was a bad deal.

Why? Why would someone call to incite such feelings of physical insecurity? Surely they knew us from the church. But we had not had time to even make any enemies. Someone was obviously not getting his or her way it seemed. But why would you try to scare a Christian woman—a young mother? Why would you seek to intimidate a son or daughter of God? We had only sought to serve God as we felt he had led us to do. We were only speaking the truth as we saw it.

Every servant of God meets with persecution, threats, or even violence. Satan, the prince of pure evil, will not—cannot—leave uncontested the one who seeks to do God's perfect bidding. "In fact, everyone who wants to live a godly life in Christ Jesus will be persecuted" (2 Tim 3:12). It is a sure thing. The only way to avoid persecution is not to live the godly life of Christ! Many traitors exist—those who may call Jesus lord, but do not do "the will of my Father who is in heaven…" To these, Jesus would say, "I never knew you. Away from me, you evildoers" (Matt 7:21–23). Generally, the world at large loves and speaks well of the false prophets, not the real ones (Luke 6:26).

We are never comfortable with this rejection and persecution. Our flesh is wired for survival. Survival involves the avoidance of making others unhappy. The greatest virtue of the Christian who has not come to fully follow Christ is to be "nice." Spiritually impotent, really. But Christ was not always "nice" in this way. And he certainly was never spiritually impotent. "Out of my sight, Satan," he'd said to Peter (Matt 16:23). That, to most of us, is just not very "nice."

The problem is that what pleases God and his true followers angers Satan. Meanwhile, what pleases Satan and those who uphold his way, God hates. "What harmony is there between Christ and Belial" (2 Cor 6:15)? You simply cannot always obey

God and be "nice," at least not by the world's standards. The world, apart from God, is determined to be told what it wants to hear, not what it needs to hear—the truth (2 Tim 4:4).

If you are possessed by God in his kingdom, you are hated by Satan. You had better deal with it—get used to it. "For our struggle is not against flesh and blood, but against the rulers, against the authorities, against the powers of this dark world and against the spiritual forces of evil in the heavenly realms" (Eph 6:12). You must be spiritually prepared.

You cannot hide the fact from Satan that you are God's. You wear a seal that is clearly visible to all the spirits in the spiritual realm (Eph 1:13). Satan knows well who your God is, and he hates you for it. Face it: serve God, and Satan will attack you.

When you are persecuted for righteousness, you can be sure Satan hates you and what you stand for. His persecution, in fact, affirms your kingdom status. His persecution comes in many forms: direct attacks of criticism, judgment, persecution, and rejection. Threats. The attacks on Christians around the world, individually and collectively, are meant to threaten and intimidate—to persecute—Christians everywhere. Similarly are the constant ugly portrayals of Christians by an unrelenting press, as well as the movie and television industry. A steady and constant eroding of Christian values and principles in society are part of the attack too. Schools are too often more congenial to atheists and Satanists than they are Christians. But "we are not unaware of his (Satan's) schemes" (2 Cor 2:11). If Satan could even use Peter against Jesus, he most certainly can use any of us, or our otherwise fine institutions.

If you are currently unresisted by Satan, or if you have never felt his heated resistance, you must examine your purposes. You must ask yourself if you are a traitor among the people of God— "away from me you evildoers" (Matt 7:22). Are you only in a lull from resistance, or are you in retreat, such that he need not attack you? You are blessed in the persecution because you are identifying with Christ, and he has promised to be with you. Paul said,

"Now I rejoice in what I am suffering for you [the Colossians], and I fill up in my flesh what is still lacking in regard to Christ's afflictions, for the sake of his body, which is the church" (Col 1:24). We finish what Christ began, and we may suffer similarly.

Look and see all the ways Satan persecutes the people of God. See who it is that society allows to be ridiculed. See who it is who gets blamed for the social ills. Calling wrong right does not make it so. God will bring truth to light in due time.

"Blessed are you when people insult you...and falsely say all kinds of evil against you because of me." Never are you closer to God than when your purposes are so conformed to his that you receive the same reception from the tempter that he did. "If the head of the house has been called Beelzebub (Satan), how much more the members of his household" (Matt 10:25). In fact, Jesus said, "Woe to you when all men speak well of you" (Luke 6:26).

Alienation, false accusations, torture, hatred, and resentment all await the soldier of the cross. Somewhere, at some point. Persecution comes in many forms, and if you become one who seeks to draw others to God, you will be subjected to these attacks of Satan. "Rejoice and be glad," because God will reward you richly (Luke 18:29–30).

"Therefore God exalted him to the highest place and gave him a name that is above every name" (Phil 2:9). A hundredfold return on investment awaits those who invest in the kingdom (Mark 10:29–30). God will repay you a hundredfold! God is able "to do more than we can ask or imagine" (Eph 3:20). Rejoice when you are counted in the lot of God.

Because you are an heir to all that God has, you are going to be persecuted in some ways at some times. However, God will richly reward you for enduring it faithfully (Eph 1:18–19).

Reflections:

1. Something to ask: Why does God allow us to suffer at the hands of Satan?

2. Something to think about: God knows your heart even when you do not even know what's going on in it. You can, however, know a lot about it by watching your own attitude and behavior when you suffer persecution, loss, or any other trouble as you live out your Christian life.

3. Something to believe: Make sure you stay on the right side, because in the end, God always wins!

4. Something to pray: Lord, help me to recognize Satan's persecution and attempts to trouble me, and help me to endure it faithfully and gracefully.

5. Something to memorize: "Blessed are those who are persecuted because of righteousness, for theirs is the kingdom of heaven" (Matt 5:10).

6. Something to do: Look for the subtle, sneaky ways that Satan and the demons persecute you. You may have seen them as the normal problems of life, when in fact they were subtle persecution.

15

Pour On the Salt

(Matt 5:13)

You are the salt of the earth. But if the salt loses its saltiness,
how can it be made salty again? It is no longer good for any-
thing, except to be thrown out and trampled by men.

Salt: a seasoning; a preservative. Sodium chloride. NaCl. To the ancients to whom Jesus originally spoke, salt had a very special significance. It was necessary for survival in several ways.

Today, salt is still used as a seasoning and preservative, but it is not as important as it was to those of the past. In fact, as with many other nutritional essentials, we often get too much of it, causing health concerns. However, we should not take salt's necessity and availability for granted, especially its value in metaphorical terms.

How literal Jesus meant to be about salt losing its saltiness is not clear. Like the water molecule, sodium chloride is one of the most stable molecules known. However, it is highly soluble in water. In discussing salt losing its saltiness, Jesus is likely speaking of the sodium chloride being dissolved out of an impure form of salt (bituminous salt) that the Jews are believed to have used in certain rituals. When water washed over it, the sodium chloride was dissolved from it and washed away, leaving only the impurities, which did not taste salty. It did not taste salty because there was no salt in it any longer. It was useless for its original purpose and had to be thrown out and replaced. Further, these impurities, if thrown on the soil, would render it infertile; thus, waste was thrown onto walkways and such, only to be trampled.

Similarly, throughout the ages, great societies have often fallen, not because of the lack of strength, but because of the lack of moral character—the lack of "salt." As evil creeps in, it at first dissolves the good and eventually washes it away, leaving only the useless waste. Without the "good," the social system is spoiled, weakened, unproductive, and eventually destroyed from within. Without people of character to preserve and protect the fibers of society against the evil onslaughts, social rotting is inevitable. What is left when the salt of society is gone is useless, comparable to the unfruitful branches that Jesus said would only be thrown into the fire (John 15:6). "You are the salt of the earth."

Many societies have risen and fallen, scarcely to be remembered, often even going unnoticed during their own times. There was no salt there, or else what was there was so diluted as to be unnoticeable. These are bland, tasteless societies that yield little in the way of blessing the world at large. It is the same with smaller social units such as families or churches. Without "salt"—those truly of Christ—these social units are at best bland and at worst are already rotting from within. They have nothing to bless others with, and in fact only have sin and corruption that will likely spill over into the world around them. Without salt within them, they are tasteless and they add nothing to their worlds.

Jesus intends for you to be salt—at home, at work, at school, and even at church. Do not allow yourself to be dissolved and washed away. Do not allow the salt within you—the Holy Spirit—to be diluted. "Do not quench the Spirit" (1 Thess 5:19). If you lose the character of God that allows you to season and preserve, you have no godly use to society. You have made your purpose yourself (Luke 9:23), or you have made your purpose the world's affairs (2 Tim 2:4). You have thus been neutralized.

If Christians have no saltiness, they deter no evil, but rather they sit benignly by as evil flourishes all around them. You can become evil yourself. We can become the destructive impurity itself—the leaven that leavens the proverbial lump (Gal 5:9). That is, if bad is left uncontested or unrivaled, it will take over. Irish author and statesman Edmund Burke said, "Evil flourishes when good men do nothing."

Do something: be bold; be strong; be assertive; be brave. Dare to act at the Spirit's bidding. Preserve faith, godliness, morality, and goodness in the world. Be like Jesus.

So pour on the salt, even if it raises the world's blood pressure a notch. "Go into all the world and preach the gospel" (Matt 28:19). It is God's way. Be salty.

Reflections:
1. Something to ask: How can I best preserve and season the world around me for God?
2. Something to think about: What might be neutralizing your own "saltiness"?
3. Something to believe: God has the power to work through you to do simple but powerful things, just as salt can do powerful things to preserve food against rotting.
4. Something to pray: Lord, help me to be the salt of the earth.
5. Something to memorize: "You are the salt of the earth. But if the salt loses its saltiness, how can it be made salty again? It is no longer good for anything, except to be thrown out and trampled by men" (Matt 5:13).
6. Something to do: Do one thing today to make the world around you a better place. Do something extra today, something that you were not going to do or that you do not normally do.

16

Lights

(Matt 5:14–16)

You are the light of the world. A city on a hill cannot be hidden.
Neither do people light a lamp and put it under a bowl. Instead
they put it on its stand, and it gives light to everyone in the house.
In the same way, let your light shine before men, that they may
see your good deeds and praise your Father in heaven.

God lit a fire on the temple altar for the children of Israel. It came down straight from heaven. All sacrifices were to be burned from it. God gave the priests the responsibility to refuel it and stoke it each morning. He told them, "The fire must not go out" (Lev 6:8–14). It was a big deal to God.

So it is with us. God puts his Spirit in our hearts as his altar fire. The Holy Spirit was often associated with fire in the scripture. When the Holy Spirit was first poured out for all humanity, falling on the apostles, it was said, "They saw what seemed to be tongues of fire that separated and came to rest on each of them. All of them were filled with the Holy Spirit" (Acts 2:3–4). We also have God's fire on our own heart altars—"You will receive the gift of the Holy Spirit" (Acts 2:38).

All our sacrifices are to be "spiritual" sacrifices, that is, to be offered and consumed by the Spirit's fire (1 Pet 2:5). That is generally how Israel knew God accepted a sacrifice to him—he consumed it with fire (1 Chr 21:26). In fact, "Our God *is* a consuming fire" (Heb 12:29). God causes his Son to be *the* "sun" and the "morning star" in our lives (2 Pet 1:19). Ours is to see by his light, be guided by his light, be warmed by his light, and to attend to his flame in our hearts on a daily basis to keep it burning brightly.

Light and darkness. God is light. Evil is darkness—the absence of light. Light is energy. In fact, light is an amazing thing in our physical world. Darkness is the absence of energy; it even inhibits and absorbs light, in a way. Light warms. Darkness cools. Light exposes and reveals. Darkness hides and obscures. Light brings security. Darkness brings fear. Light awakens. Darkness makes us sleepy. Light brings hope. Darkness brings hopelessness. Good flourishes and grows in the light. Evil flourishes and grows in the darkness.

God has planted us, his children, in the world as lights—streetlights and lighthouses and flashlights and searchlights and reading lights. Lights to light our driveways and highways, our walkways and waterways. Lights to search for the lost and those in trouble. Beacons. God has planted his children in the world to radiate light—his light—to everyone, even those that do not know him. "He causes his sun to rise on the evil and the good, and sends rain on the righteous and the unrighteous" (Matt 5:45).

God wants his lights raised so others may see him through them. "A city on a hill cannot be hid." And "a lamp…on its stand…gives light to everyone in the house." God wants all people to be able to see, rather than to live blindly in darkness. God wants our lights to shine brightly for them. "Be aglow with the Spirit" (Rom 12:11, Revised Standard Version).

Light brings glory to God. The Holy Spirit within us is the source of all spiritual light. Our right living and good deeds are light. God wants them done in his name in order to align the world rightly with their loving Father—"that they may see your good deeds, and praise your Father in heaven." And, "we are

God's workmanship created in Christ Jesus to do good works" (Eph 2:10). We are created to do good works—to be light.

What is it that God is just now inspiring you to do? Where is his Spirit trying to lead you that you may not be going? What has he specially gifted you to do? What is it you have seemingly "always wanted to do," for goodness' sake—for God's sake? Do it. Do it soon. Do it now. Just start. Go stand by the chariot, as Philip did (Acts 8:29). Good things will happen. You do not have to even know the next step. The words or actions "will be given you" (Matt 10:19). You show up for God, and God will show up for you. He is always faithful!

And do not be so afraid of stealing glory from God when you do good deeds. You are his, and thus everything you do is his work—"it is God who works in you to will and to act in order to fulfill his good purpose" (Phil 2:13). Just give him credit at every turn (1 Cor 15:10). "Whatever you do, whether in word or deed, do it all in the name of the Lord Jesus, giving thanks to God the Father through him" (Col 3:17). And, "whatever you do, work at it with all your heart, as working for the Lord, not for men" (Col 3:23). Give glory to God. Of course, work in secret as much as possible in order to please him and so as to receive a reward only from him (Matt 6:3–4). Others will see the results of the good you do, but they will not see you; they will see him—much better for them *and* for you. "Your Father, who sees what is done in secret, will reward you" (Matt 6:4). But do not be afraid. God will sanctify your good deeds for his purposes and work out your deeds and even your mistakes to conform to his sovereign will (Rom 8:28; Eph 1:11).

Build your house in a community on a hill—the kind of church that Christ wants. Plug in your lamps. Turn on all the lights in your house. Have an "every light on" block party. You and everyone else, open your doors and windows and let the light of Christ in your life flood the streets with his glow—with his glory. Turn on your searchlights and be about his mission of seeking and saving the lost. Aim the reflector of your heart on the world around you and let him bounce off to light up others. Live on a hill. Ever be on a lamp stand. Be aglow with the Spirit of God so others can see. And give praises to God!

Reflections:
1. Something to ask: What is it that might be dimming or obscuring God's light, keeping it from shining from me?
2. Something to think about: The power and energy is from him, not from me. This is not something that I contrive or create; it is something I reflect when I spend time with him (2 Cor 3:18).
3. Something to believe: God can shine from me through both my strengths *and* my weaknesses (2 Cor 12:9–10). Do not be afraid to shine.
4. Something to pray: God, may your pure, unadulterated, unobscured light shine from my life in order to show your glory.
5. Something to memorize: "Let your light shine before men, that they may see your good deeds and praise your Father in heaven" (Matt 5:16).
6. Something to do: Think of how other disciples have shone the light of Christ in your life in special or unique ways. Imitate them.

17

Don't Confuse the Issue

(Matt 5:17–20)

Do not think that I have come to abolish the Law or the Prophets; I have not come to abolish them but to fulfill them. I tell you the truth, until heaven and earth disappear, not the smallest letter, not the least stroke of a pen, will by any means disappear from the Law until everything is accomplished. Anyone who breaks one of the least of these commandments and teaches others to do the same will be called least in the kingdom of heaven, but whoever practices and teaches these commands will be called great in the kingdom of heaven. For I tell you that unless your righteousness surpasses that of the Pharisees and the teachers of the law, you will certainly not enter the kingdom of heaven.

"I have not come to abolish the Law or the Prophets; I have come to fulfill them." The law was the teacher designed to bring us to Christ (Gal 3:24). It was, and still is, the "Tree of the Knowledge of Good and Evil." Adam and Eve had chosen it. Its selection as the path for humankind was the original sin. The Law was, however, not bad, but good (Rom 7:10–13). But it was not a good choice for us, because we cannot have a relationship with a holy God by our own merit and attainment (Gal 3:21). "Clearly, no one is justified before God [saved] by law" (Gal 3:11).

The Law could not make us righteous because we could not keep it—we cannot keep it. Or any just law. Not completely. Not perfectly. God's old covenant with Israel was nullified because God found fault in the people's inability to keep their part of the bargain: "God found fault with the people" (Heb 8:8). The Law only reveals our own personal unrighteousness (Rom 3:23).

Righteousness in Christ's way means "being right with God." *By law* this is impossible for mortal man, because to be right with God in this way, we cannot break even one law once! There has to be another choice if any of us are to be saved—another way: "the righteousness that comes from God and is by faith" (Phil 3:9). Paul understood it. All the prophets, including Paul, lived out their prophecies. They mostly experienced in many ways what they wrote about (see Hosea). Paul lived out the grace experience. God expressed his grace through Paul—an enemy of Christ and the cross—a self-righteous Pharisee, taken to his knees and reduced to a blind heap of confusion (Acts 9). "The least of the apostles" (1 Cor 15:9), the "worst sinner" (1 Tim 1:15), and "the end of the procession" (1 Cor. 4:9), Paul called himself. The least, the worst, and the last. He said, "But by the grace of God I am what I am, and his grace to me was not without effect. No, I worked harder than all of them—yet not I, but the grace of God that was with me" (1 Cor 15:10). Paul of course understood, and explained as well, that one is not saved BY works, however he did point out that one is indeed saved FOR works (Eph. 2:8-10).

As had their original mother and father—Eve and Adam—missed the message of the two trees, Israel had missed the point of the law—the "tree in the midst of the garden." Therefore they had missed the point about righteousness. Righteousness, "rightness" with God, could not be attained by sinful men. "For whoever keeps the whole law and yet stumbles at just one point is guilty of breaking all of it" (James 2:10).

The Law and the Prophets were pointing ahead to *the* righteousness from God—Jesus (Rom 1:16–17). The fulfillment of the Law and the Prophets is *the* righteousness. *He* fulfilled them. And in him, we fulfill them. "He condemned sin in sinful man, in order that the righteous requirements of the law might be fully met in us" (Rom 8:4). "That in him we might become the righteousness of God" (2 Cor 5:21).

You will not be able to outdo the scribes and Pharisees in acts of religion and piety. Do not even try. Rather, "out believe" them. The righteousness of God is by faith. In Christ, God *sees* us as holy and blameless (Eph 1:4). We are not righteous within ourselves, but he sees us that way anyway. He calls things that are not as though they are (Rom 4:17). He calls us "holy and blameless" when we, in fact, are not.

Do not miss the point. Israel was the house of God in the Old Testament, the nation of his promise. Israel was his covenant people. To her was given the Law and the Prophets. Through her, the promised Messiah came.

Yet, Israel missed the real point about righteousness. "Since they did not know the righteousness that comes from God and sought to establish their own, they did not submit to God's righteousness. Christ is the end of the law so that there may be righteousness for everyone who believes" (Rom 10:3).

Let your righteousness in Christ far exceed that of any attempted "law-keeping." This applies to keeping any law, whether the Law of Moses or some "law" contrived by humans, be it a "Christian" law or otherwise. Do not let anyone put such a yoke of burden on you. Know and believe that your "righteousness" comes not by your own attainment or achievement, but by his mercy and atonement. Do not confuse the issues of law and righteousness. Have faith in Christ and find true righteousness.

Do not ever allow yourself to be confused about the basis of your right-relationship with God. If you allow it to happen, you will alienate yourself from Christ himself (Gal 5:4).

Reflections:

1. Something to ask: Why am I so prone to try to attain salvation rather than accept the grace of Christ?

2. Something to think about: Just as the prophets lived out the realities of what they were prophesying, we often must live out what God is teaching us.

3. Something to believe: God designed from the beginning to see us as perfect—holy and blameless—as we believe and live in Christ.

4. Something to pray: God, grant me the faith to live a life of trust in your goodness and grace.

5. Something to memorize: "For I tell you that unless your righteousness surpasses that of the Pharisees and the teachers of the law, you will certainly not enter the kingdom of heaven" (Matt 5:20).

6. Something to do: Spend some time pondering the things that you "do" that might be making you fear for your right relationship to God. Next, spend some time thinking about things that you do that might make you feel more secure in your salvation. Now write out an explanation of why, if you live by faith in Christ, the former cannot condemn you and the latter cannot actually "save" you.

18

Deal with It

(Matt 5:21–26)

You have heard that it was said to the people long ago, "Do not murder, and anyone who murders will be subject to judgment." But I tell you that anyone who is angry with his brother will be subject to judgment. Again, anyone who says to his brother, "Raca," is answerable to the Sanhedrin. But anyone who says, "You fool!" will be in danger of the fire of hell. Therefore, if you are offering your gift at the altar and there remember that your brother has something against you, leave your gift there in front of the altar. First go and be reconciled to your brother; then come and offer your gift. Settle matters quickly with your adversary who is taking you to court. Do it while you are still with him on the way, or he may hand you over to the judge, and the judge may hand you over to the officer, and you may be thrown into prison. I tell you the truth, you will not get out until you have paid the last penny.

The religious leaders tried to trap Jesus, asking, "Teacher, which is the greatest commandment in the law?" Jesus replied, "Love the Lord your God with all of your heart with all of your soul and with all of your mind" (Matt 22:37). Further, he said, "Love your neighbor as yourself" (Matt 22:39). Neither of these statements was actually one of the Ten Commandments, the basis of the law to which they were referring, and likely the specific list of commandments they were asking about. However, Moses had indeed given them as a summary statement (Deut 6:5–6), much as Jesus had summarized his Sermon on the Mount in a similar fashion (Matt 7:12). So Jesus threw his inquisitors off. They wanted to argue but instead got another difficult tutorial in truth.

It seems they had missed the whole point of the Law. Wow. How had they done that? "You have neglected the more important matters of the law—justice, mercy and faithfulness" (Matt 23:23). The Law revealed the Lawgiver. But they had gotten a "law" without getting the lawgiver. They got the rule, but not the intent of the rule. Consequently, they seemingly misapplied the rule as well, more often than not.

The point is relationships. You got the "do not kill" part, but you missed the part about having a right attitude toward a brother. Harboring anger and then allowing the subsequent bitterness to spread toward another is to murder him or her within yourself. "In your anger do not sin. Do not let the sun go down while you are still angry, and do not give the devil a foothold" (Eph 4:26–27). "Man's anger does not bring about the righteous life that God desires" (James 1:20). Rather, man's anger, unresolved, gives a foothold to the evil one.

Therefore, learn not just to resist physically taking another's life or murdering them with your tongue, resist killing them within yourself by harboring resentment and anger. In addition, do all you can to prevent another from harboring anger against you. If in your worship times with God you are reminded or shown that another is angry with you, go be reconciled to them. Then worship. "As far as it depends on you, live at peace with everyone" (Rom 12:18).

Learn to deal with your anger as well with the anger of others. Do not take anger lightly, as it is a foothold of the devil. It does not bring about the work of God but rather destroys it. Anger should be for us an emotional alarm—a signal that something is wrong. When you hear it go off, turn the alarm off first—cool off—so that the noise does not just add to your frustration. "In your anger, do not sin." Then, deal with what is wrong. And definitely, do not leave the alarm on lest the alarm itself cause greater damage than the original problem.

"See to it that no one misses the grace of God and that no bitter root grows up to cause trouble and defile many" (Heb 12:15). Face off with your anger. Focus on resolving the source of it before your anger becomes its own source, and a vicious cycle of bitterness and malice takes root in your heart.

So deal with it—your anger, that is.

Reflections:

1. Something to ask: What is the godly purpose for anger?
2. Something to think about: Consider how many of your hurts have been caused more by the anger surrounding a hurtful relationship or event than by any damage the actual event caused.
3. Something to believe: Anger unresolved leads to sin and serious damage.
4. Something to pray: Lord, help me to become one who deals effectively every day with my anger, as well as others' anger involving me.
5. Something to memorize: "Therefore, if you are offering your gift at the altar and there remember that your brother has something against you, leave your gift there in front of the altar. First go and be reconciled to your brother; then come and offer your gift" (Matt 5:23–24).
6. Something to do: Make a list of those who have made you angry. Make a list of those who may have been angry with you. Make a note by each of these what you might need to do to rectify situations and reconcile relationships.

19

Adultery of the Heart

(Matt 5:27–30)

You have heard that it was said, "Do not commit adultery." But I tell you that anyone who looks at a woman lustfully has already committed adultery with her in his heart. If your right eye causes you to sin, gouge it out and throw it away. It is better for you to lose one part of your body than for your whole body to be thrown into hell. And if your right hand causes you to sin, cut it off and throw it away. It is better for you to lose one part of your body than for your whole body to go into hell.

Relationships begin in the head and in the heart. Marriage is such a relationship. Thus, what we actually end up doing only reflects who we are inside our heads and hearts. To say "I have not had sexual relations with a member of the opposite sex, other than my mate," is good, but what about inwardly? Am I inwardly faithful? To my mate? What do you think your mate would say if she or he had been able to read your actual thoughts all this time? What about your relationship to God? And he *can* read your thoughts (Jer 17:10).

I may show up at the church building every time the doors open. As part of the bride of Christ, the church, I may commune with God faithfully in my quiet times, meditations, and corporate worship times, all while my gazes wander lustfully toward the world. "No one can serve two masters...You cannot serve both God and Money" (Matt 6:24).

The legalistic interpretation of the law that focuses on the external is worldly. "The Lord does not look at the things man looks at. Man looks at the outward appearance, but the Lord looks at the heart" (1 Sam 16:7). You can fool man, but you cannot fool God. How foolish it is to try.

God does not really have to look at what you're doing. He knows what you are up to by the condition of your heart and mind. His Spirit lives in the hearts of Christians. "Out of the overflow of the heart the mouth speaks" (Matt 12:34). It is through his Spirit that God lives in us, searches our hearts, and interacts with us directly (Rom 8:27).

Jesus said, "First clean the inside of the cup and dish, and then the outside also will be clean" (Matt 23:26). Since God looks at the heart, and it is he we aim to please, should we not first be concerned with cleaning the heart? Jesus says that, in cleaning out the heart (the inside of the cup and dish), we will clean the outside also.

"You are already clean because of the word I have spoken to you" (John 15:3). God's word is his cleansing agent for his children. We are made clean "by the washing with water through the word" (Eph 5:26). "It (God's word) judges the thoughts and attitudes of the heart" (Heb 4:12). It reveals to us what ought to go and what ought to stay, and it grows within us to accomplish that purpose.

The word forces us to remove that part of our lives that offends—eyes, hands, and whatever else offends. What idols have you set up in your life to cast your lustful eye toward? Is it your possessions? Is it a person or persons? Is it a position? Is it an ambition? In what purposes and activities other than God's do your hands involve themselves? The first of the Ten Commandments: "You shall have no other gods before me" (Exod 20:3).

For the sake of heaven and for the avoidance of hell, we must remove those parts of ourselves that are attracted to anything that offends God—that adulterates our relationships to him—especially regarding our sexual and marital faithfulness that are at the core and foundation of individuals and societies. Simply offering outward observance is not enough. God is looking at you inwardly. It is within your heart that you prove faithful, and it is within your heart that the real adultery occurs.

A covenant is a formal agreement between two or more individuals or groups. Marriage is one of the most sacred, God-given covenants of humankind. And it is God who joins a man and a woman together in a marriage covenant—"Therefore what God has joined together, let no one separate" (Matt 19:6). God is a God of covenants—"Know therefore that the Lord your God is God; he is the faithful God, keeping his covenant of love to a thousand generations of those who love him and keep his commandments" (Deut 7:9). God keeps his covenants, and he expects us to keep ours—"When you make a vow to God, do not delay to fulfill it. He has no pleasure in fools; fulfill your vow" (Eccl 5:4).

Can God forgive our adulteries? Of course—over and over again. But should God's willingness to forgive, enable or entitle us to pursue our illicit lusts? Of course not! God's grace is not extended to us just to forgive us our sins; it goes far beyond that to teach us to avoid them! "For the grace of God has appeared that offers salvation to all people. It teaches us to say 'no' to ungodliness and worldly passions, and to live self-controlled, upright and godly lives in this present age" (Titus 2:11–12). God's love and grace teaches us to say "no" to those things that most harm us. Adultery in any form, physical and/or emotional, but especially of the marital variety, is harmful. God loves us enough to teach us to say "no" to it. Rather, God's love teaches us to trust him, and to say "yes" to him.

Reflections:

1. Something to ask: What thoughts actually constitute lust? When do evil desires and impurities become actual lust?

2. Something to think about: How can a person gain greater control over evil thoughts that lead to lust?

3. Something to believe: Faithfulness and fidelity are extremely important to God.

4. Something to pray: O Lord, help me to become faithful in all my covenants.

5. Something to memorize: "I tell you that anyone who looks at a woman lustfully has already committed adultery with her in his heart" (Matt 5:28).

6. Something to do: Look around your home, car, and work area. What things might be lying around that provoke lustful thoughts, be they sexual or covetous in nature? Determine which ones you might need to get rid of.

20

Dear John?—Not Such a Good Idea

(Matt 5:31–32)

It has been said, "Anyone who divorces his wife must give her a certificate of divorce." But I tell you that anyone who divorces his wife, except for marital unfaithfulness, causes her to become an adulteress, and anyone who marries the divorced woman commits adultery.

"Is it lawful for a man to divorce his wife for any and every reason?" they asked Jesus. These who were so knowledgeable about the scripture—these Pharisees who sought to "routinize" every line of scripture into a specific, physically "obeyable," obligatory rule—they were the ones asking.

"Haven't you read?" Jesus retorted. Have you read the whole Bible and missed the point? "What God has joined together, let man not separate" (Matt 19:6).

But, they asked, "Why, then, did Moses command that a man give his wife a certificate of divorce and send her away?" (Matt 19:7).

"Because *your* hearts were hard. But it was not this way from the beginning" (Matt 19:8). Jesus knew they were not getting it. They never had. They were really clueless. They were not even "warm," so to speak. They were on the wrong side of the room, looking for a right relationship with God. Leave them alone, he said to his disciples (Matt 15:14).

Jesus was not really talking just about marriage here. He was talking about the principle of commitment in relationships. Principles and rules are not altered by possible exceptions. Looking here at the exception—"except for marital unfaithfulness"—is to miss the rule. That Moses gave permission misses the point.

You have focused on the escape chute—"give her a certificate of divorce"—and missed the meaning of relationship. Breaking a relationship through marital infidelity adulterates that relationship. What is adulterated is adulterated.

To violate relationships by harboring even the possibility of divorce in your heart is to adulterate that relationship from within—"he has already committed adultery." What "has been said," speaking of the Jew's oral tradition, was just not really "right" in God's eyes. And if you cannot get it about earthly marriage, how will you ever get being the bride of Christ?

Take "divorce" out of your "spell check" and "thesaurus." If you later need an exception to some rule, God will show you the way out. Until then, forget about it.

It is not over till it is over. No "Dear John letters" allowed.

Reflections:
1. Something to ask: Do I seek to assure I always have a way out even of the most sacred of relationships?
2. Something to think about: By seeking to understand God's grace toward those who are divorced, we might have missed the deeper issues of faithfulness.
3. Something to believe: Faithfulness is a greater virtue than happiness.
4. Something to pray: Help me, O God, to have wisdom to understand your purposes in marriage as well as all covenant relationships.
5. Something to memorize: "It has been said, 'Anyone who divorces his wife must give her a certificate of divorce.' But I tell you that anyone who divorces his wife, except

for marital unfaithfulness, causes her to become an adulteress, and anyone who marries the divorced woman commits adultery" (Matt 5:31–32).

6. Something to do: Write a note to a couple of married couples who have exemplary marriages to encourage them and let them know that you have been strengthened by their marital example of faithfulness.

21

Don't Swear

(Matt 5:33–37)

Again, you have heard that it was said to the people long ago, "Do not break your oath, but keep the oaths you have made to the Lord." But I tell you, Do not swear at all: either by heaven, for it is God's throne; or by the earth, for it is his footstool; or by Jerusalem, for it is the city of the Great King. And do not swear by your head, for you cannot make even one hair white or black. Simply let your "Yes" be "Yes," and your "No," "No"; anything beyond this comes from the evil one.

Jesus *was* what he spoke about. Jesus *spoke* about what he was. Jesus was *the Word* (John 1:1). The discourse referred to as "the Sermon on the Mount" was revealing how Israel, in her focus on the ability to translate principles to rules and rules to rigorous obedience, missed the Rule-Giver. They found the revelation, but not the Revelator.

What does making a "promise" or a "vow" or an "oath" have to say about the other things you say without such qualifications? Are they less true? Is a "promise" you make truer than other things you say?

Sincerity is about being the same on the inside and the outside. Integrity is about being an integrated whole—the same through and through—without apparent contradictions. To be a person of sincerity and integrity is to be completely honest. If one is completely honest, there is no need for promises, vows, or oaths.

If we swear by something else, does that make this truer than the "average" promise? If we swear by something of God, does that make it a "super" promise? What about if we "cross our hearts and hope to die" (better not tempt others this way)? The answer is no. All these vows and promises do is bring into question all your other commitments.

If you say you will do it, do it. If you say you will not do something, do not. Keep it simple. Yes. No.

Jesus told a story about two sons. He told them to go work in the vineyard. One said he would do it and did not. The other said he would not do it and then did. Jesus asked which of the two sons was actually obedient to their father (Matt 21:28–32). The Jews who were being challenged got the answer to Jesus's question in the story correct. However, Jesus goes on to explain that they, in fact, were as the son who said he would go and then did not. In this case, their yes was really "no."

Practice thinking first what the truth inside of you really is. You must first be honest with yourself before you can truly be honest with others. As Polonius said in the line from Hamlet, "This above all: to thine own self be true, And it must follow, as the night the day, Thou canst not then be false to any man" (*Hamlet*, Act 1, Scene 3). If you are honest with God, you will be honest with yourself. If you are honest with yourself, you will be honest with others.

Make it your habit to speak only the truth, without compromise, and without any qualifying promises or oaths.

Speak who you are, and be who you say you are. "Yes." Or, "no." Sufficient answers for one of integrity.

Do not swear. The person of God should not need to.

Reflections:
1. Something to ask: Am I an honest person? Can I be trusted in all or at all?

2. Something to think about: If you will lie about anything, you will lie about *anything*.

3. Something to believe: You must simply say what you will do and do what you say. Period.

4. Something to pray: God, help me to stand always on the side of truth. Help me to be truth so that I will tell the truth.

5. Something to memorize: "Simply let your 'Yes' be 'Yes,' and your 'No,' 'No'; anything beyond this comes from the evil one" (Matt 5:37).

6. Something to do: Practice truth today. Before you speak or write, simply ask yourself, "Is it the truth, the whole truth, not an exaggeration either way, and nothing but the truth?"

22

Getting Even

(Matt 5:38–42)

You have heard that it was said, "Eye for eye, and tooth for tooth." But I tell you, do not resist an evil person. If someone strikes you on the right cheek, turn to him the other also. And if someone wants to sue you and take your tunic, let him have your cloak as well. If someone forces you to go one mile, go with him two miles. Give to the one who asks you, and do not turn away from the one who wants to borrow from you.

Those that do not know God try to dominate and control their own lives. The world is set up with a one-over-the-other structure. "Not so with you...whoever wants to become great among you must be your servant" (Matt 20:26). The kingdom of God is simply opposite of the kingdom of this world. It is upside down.

The purpose of the law in this regard was not to command an "in-kind" retribution, but rather it was to limit any retribution to in-kind. But fallen humans use that kind of limitation against going too far in retribution as an excuse to get revenge.

The kingdom of God is to be different. In the kingdom, leaders will be servants, and servants will be leaders. The first go last, and the last go first. The rich are poor and the poor are rich. The humble get exalted and the exalted get humbled. We give expecting nothing in return. We suffer harm without harming back. Christians recognize themselves as the least, the last, the lowest, and the worst. "Honor one another above yourselves" (Rom 12:10). In that reality, we discover who we really are! And it is really quite beautiful. Do you think you get this?

How are you going to handle those who treat you unfairly? Jesus saw the evil injustice of slavery. Yet, he never led a "free-the-slaves" protest. He saw the oppression of women and the plight of children, but he never had the apostles begin a campaign for women's or children's rights. Not directly anyway. Indirectly, though, he led the greatest movement ever possible against such as these—"As I have loved you, so you must love one another" (John 13:34).

Jesus taught them how "to inherit the earth." He taught slaves and women and children how to overcome it all. He taught how to live above it. If you get in a "tit-for-tat" contest with the world, you are playing the game on Satan's terms and turf. "Do not take revenge, my friends, but leave room for God's wrath, for it is written: 'It is mine to avenge; I will repay,' says the Lord" (Rom 12:19).

Perhaps no other words of Christ are more controversial. Biblical interpretation comes from humans beings though, and yielding to aggressive people is not "natural," especially to most males, who have up to now done most of the interpreting. Hence, the spirit of this text is arguably one of the most violated principles of the Bible. Just as with the Pharisees, those who claim to be most committed to a rigid view of the Bible and its strict application are often the most adept at justifying ignoring it—at disobeying it—"Not everyone who says to me, 'Lord, Lord,' will enter the kingdom of heaven, but only he who does the will of my Father who is in heaven" (Matt 7:21).

Should one not protect oneself, loved ones, and possessions? Should we allow another to violate us and rob us of our dignity? Give him your coat also!

Whose are we, anyway? Should we not look to see how God wants *his* property handled? Should we not check out our owner's manual? Does it matter what I want or what I think?

"Do not *resist* an evil person." Not very comfortable is it? Get the feel. Notice how your flesh does not like it. Say it out loud. Now go ahead. Say, "But…"

"Turn the other cheek." This one does not sit well either, does it? But what about our rights? What rights? Did you not surrender your "rights" to God? "You are not your own; you were bought at a price. Therefore honor God with your body" (1 Cor 6:19–20). Thus, to what are you entitled? Happiness? Safety? Comfort? If Jesus is the model (and for Christians, he is), the answer to whether you can expect each of these and others is, "not necessarily."

"Yet it was the Lord's will to crush him and cause him to suffer" (Isa 53:10). The Father did love his Son. Yet he willed him to suffer and be crushed. For a very good reason, of course. A "pop to both chops" is no big deal compared to what God let happen to *the* Son, now is it?

Kingdom living means trusting God to work out his will in every way. God's ways of doing things are radically different than the world's ways (Isa 55:8–9). God simply does not do things "naturally," so don't be looking in your own head for how to react to unfair and evil behavior. "Do not rely on your own understanding" (Prov 3:5).

In fact, give the evil man extra—your clothes plus your overcoat, an extra mile, an extra dollar. Do not play his game. Do not get on his game board. Do not get on his turf. Think the "kingdom" way, not the world's way.

If you let anyone, especially an evil person, cause you to do something, you are being driven by Satan. "Out of my sight, Satan! You are a stumbling block to me: you do not have in mind the things of God, but the things of men" (Matt 16:23). Jesus said these words to Peter when Peter tried to deter him from going to Jerusalem to "suffer many things…[and] be killed" (Matt 16:21). Can you blame Peter? Would any of us do differently with one we loved? There will always be people who will help us justify doing the humanly reasonable thing—"you've got to look out for yourself!" There will always be one to justify our resisting an evil person. But do not listen. Listen to the truth. Listen to Jesus.

You see, Jesus was going the extra mile, turning the other cheek, and not resisting an evil man—just like he commanded. He was what he said.

A hawk or a dove—which are you? Perhaps if we resolve our anger quickly, as commanded, and seek to reconcile ourselves to those angry with us even before we worship, like Jesus said, and go into all the world and make disciples, like he said, we would not have to worry so much about fighting or about war anyway.

Let God protect you. Let God use you. In pleasure and in pain. In victory and in defeat.

Reflections:

1. Something to ask: Are Jesus's words here a complete condemnation of self-defense and war, even gross injustices against humanity? If not, then what is the context that necessitates protective behaviors?

2. Something to think about: Perhaps the first question in determining a course of action is not *what* it is about, but *whom*. Am I making it about me?

3. Something to believe: You can never do exactly as Jesus would do until you are exactly who Jesus was.

4. Something to pray: Lord, help my desire to please you always override my desire to please me.

5. Something to memorize: "You have heard that it was said, 'Eye for eye, and tooth for tooth.' But I tell you, do not resist an evil person" (Matt 5:38–39).

6. Something to do: Search your heart to see if you are presently resenting or hoping for hurt or harm against anyone. Are you behaving in some passive-aggressive way toward another? The other might not know it, but God does. Perhaps you are behaving badly toward others at work. Perhaps with your mate or a family member. Ask the Spirit to help you see it and to convict you of it. Pray for this person's well-being. Pray for forgiveness. Pray for freedom from Satan's control in it.

23

Friends and Enemies

(Matt 5:43–48)

You have heard that it was said, "Love your neighbor and hate your enemy." But I tell you: Love your enemies and pray for those who persecute you, that you may be sons of your Father in heaven. He causes his sun to rise on the evil and the good, and sends rain on the righteous and the unrighteous. If you love those who love you, what reward will you get? Are not even the tax collectors doing that? And if you greet only your brothers, what are you doing more than others? Do not even pagans do that? Be perfect, therefore, as your heavenly Father is perfect.

The Jews to whom Jesus spoke had heard "love your neighbor" *read*, but they had only heard "hate your enemies" *said*. The latter had simply not been written in the scripture; it was a part of their oral tradition. Thinking like humans, though, to them it just seemed to follow. Some have justified various practices not specifically condemned by scripture by pointing out that it does not say *not* to do something. That is supposed to make it all right—at least by human logic, I suppose. We are not to use the human perspective, though. "From now on we regard no one from a worldly point of view" (2 Cor 5:16).

Even the wicked are capable of loving their own. If you want to be good in human terms, imitate "good" humans. If you want to be like God, you will have to be different from most in this world, even "good" people. In fact, in being like God, you will too often be the opposite of even the supposed "good" people. "I never knew you," Jesus will ultimately say to some allegedly good people (Matt 7:23). Speaking of life as God knows it, Jesus said, "Only a few find it" (Matt 7:13–14). God is *so* very different from the darkness of the world. So *very* different. "As the heavens are higher than the earth, so are my ways higher than your ways and my thoughts than your thoughts" (Isa 55:9).

God gives sunshine and rain to both the righteous and the unrighteous—he blesses his whole creation similarly. Now, if you want to be a son of God—to be like God—you will have to change your ways and *be* like him. It does not have to make sense to you; it just has to be right, like God. It has to make sense to him!

Christ is the model. He is the archetype. He is what I heard a sage once say "done right looks like." He is the mold. If he loves his enemies, then you love yours. No excuses.

Perfection. "Be perfect as your Father in heaven is perfect." "Be imitators of God, therefore, as dearly loved children" (Eph 5:1). Focus on the Father—who he is, what he is, how he does it, why he does it, and to whom he does it. Do life as your Father does life. Be perfect AS the Father is perfect, because he defines perfect.

Aim for perfection—aim to be like the Father. Jesus: "Anyone who has seen me has seen the Father" (John 14:9). Be perfect.

Reflections:
1. Something to ask: How can we strive for godly perfection without becoming self-righteous and legalistic, and thus lose our faith in his grace and goodness?
2. Something to think about: We must first decide which measuring stick we'll use to determine who our friends and enemies are.
3. Something to believe: Just because not all will be *your* friends does not mean you cannot be a friend to all.

4. Something to pray: Lord, help me grow beyond selfish human interests that drive me to judge others by their possible benefit or detriment to me.

5. Something to memorize: "I tell you: Love your enemies and pray for those who persecute you, that you may be sons of your Father in heaven" (Matt 5:44–45).

6. Something to do: Determine whom you would consider your own personal greatest enemies and the greatest enemies of your country, as well as Christianity itself. Now pray for them. Honestly and sincerely pray for their well-being. Pray that God continues to bless them and that he judges them in mercy, not in wrath.

24

Don't Be a Show-Off

(Matt 6:1–4)

Be careful not to do your "acts of righteousness" before men, to be seen by them. If you do, you will have no reward from your Father in heaven. So when you give to the needy, do not announce it with trumpets, as the hypocrites do in the synagogues and on the streets, to be honored by men. I tell you the truth, they have received their reward in full. But when you give to the needy, do not let your left hand know what your right hand is doing, so that your giving may be in secret. Then your Father, who sees what is done in secret, will reward you.

"Be careful." Be full of care and concern about this. "Take careful consideration about what I am about to tell you," says Jesus. Jesus framed a number his statements with such—"truly, truly, I say to you." This is very important; he wanted them (us) to know.

Do not do what you are supposed to do for God in order to impress people. You will get your reward from whomever you seek to impress—God or human. You have to choose. Others cannot immediately tell what your motives are. God can, though. He looks at the heart. If you try to impress others, you will do what you do, as well as the way in which you do it, according to what others want. You will, of course, avoid embarrassment and persecution. You will avoid displeasing other people. And you will also end up doing the opposite of what God wants you to do!

False religion is mostly about trying to impress others—and using God's way as a means to do so. False teachers lead you to them, not to him (Jesus). Jesus becomes the excuse for doing things rather than the reason for doing them. God does not take well to that. Who would?

I heard someone say once that character is who you are when nobody is looking. That resonates with me. It tests me. Who am I when nobody else is looking?

I remember one time years ago driving home from church on a four-lane street. There were these people in a convertible just cruising along. I was going a little faster than they were as we went through this intersection. In the Phoenix suburb where we lived at the time, there were not many storm drains as there was not much rain, and so the roads were shaped so that water drained beside the road. Well, the road we were crossing was arched upward so that once you went over it, you drove into a low area for drainage. There was water standing in this one. When I hit the water, it sprayed all over the people in the convertible driving in the lane next to me! I didn't even realize it, but I would very soon!

In the car were a couple of very yuppie Phoenix suburbanites probably going home from Sunday brunch and enjoying a pleasant Arizona Sunday. I had splashed their designer duds *and* their cool convertible. Well, they immediately sped up and shouted… let's say, "unfriendly" things at me, as well as making unfriendly gestures with their hands. My children were watching carefully as these grown-ups made complete fools of themselves. I really felt badly, as I would never in a million years have done something like that on purpose. Well, maybe in a million years if I was not in a good place, but you know what I mean. I'm not that way. The timing had been perfect, though, for giving them a nice shower. I doubt I could have done it on purpose if I had tried over and over. It was totally an accident, and if they had thought about it, they would have known that for sure. They did not think about it; they just reacted.

I saw them turn off into a neighborhood near our house, and feeling badly myself, and as well wanting to teach my kids a lesson, I turned around and went down their street. Their car was easy to spot, and they were still out there in the driveway. I turned in, and they looked like deer in the headlights. I am sure they were expecting a fight, but I got out and just said how sorry I was for what had happened, that it was totally an accident, and I would like to have their car and clothes cleaned and so forth. These were mannerly people who were apologetic themselves at that point, but their reactions had betrayed their "nice" exteriors and revealed their darker sides—a side we all, in fact, possess. We all have one. We can all act that way. Especially when we just react to something negative. I have been on their side of such an exchange, where my behavior betrayed me to others, but it is so much easier to see it in others than in ourselves.

Jesus said what was inside was what would come out. And you can fool everyone but God; hence his encouragement to clean the inside of yourself first (Matt 23:26). What is inside of you—inside your heart and your mind?

The Pharisees take a beating in the gospels. And I guess they deserved it. Sadly, I relate to them a lot, though. Most of us can if we are honest with ourselves. It is easy just to learn to "do the right thing" and then just go do it. We "go to church," but are we even "there"? We say "please" and "thank you," but are we thankful? We treat the neighbors in a friendly way, even if we do not like them and if we talk ugly about them behind their backs, but do we care about their well-being? We even like the feeling of seeing the faces of those we serve. And we secretly bask in the praise others heap on us when we serve. But why?

When we do good things to be seen by people, God knows it is not being done for him. It is really in the motive. Why did you do it? If you do it for God, you will want as little attention and fanfare as possible, and if you get any, only enough that others will know it is because of your faith in Jesus. If you do it for you, you will want to do a public relations release for the local paper concerning this new, awesome ministry you have personally started. You will want your name on a brick or the side of a building. Perhaps you will want a picture of yourself and one of the less fortunate so blessed by you on a billboard!

You get my drift?

Focus on God, and you will not focus on humanity or yourself. Focus on God, and you will want to please God. When it comes to the things of God, do not be a show-off.

Reflections:
1. Something to ask: How can we let our lights shine for God and still do what we do in secret for God?
2. Something to think about: Being able to do good for God without others knowing about it is one of the greatest tests of the strength of our faith.
3. Something to believe: God is always watching. As a loving, caring parent with a child, God is always aware of our doings. And he is so proud of us when we do things well and for the right reasons.
4. Something to pray: Lord, help me to do what I do for you and you alone, and to always remember that in doing so, I am doing what is ultimately best for everyone else.
5. Something to memorize: "Be careful not to do your 'acts of righteousness' before men, to be seen by them. If you do, you will have no reward from your Father in heaven" (Matt 6:1).
6. Something to do: Do something extravagantly generous for someone who really needs it, making sure only God will ever know. Do not let it slip out or hint to others. Nobody must have a clue! Keep it just between you and God—the one you seek to please in it.

25

Don't Show Off, but Do Give to the Needy

(Matt 6:1–4)

Be careful not to do your "acts of righteousness" before men, to be seen by them. If you do, you will have no reward from your Father in heaven. So when you give to the needy, do not announce it with trumpets, as the hypocrites do in the synagogues and on the streets, to be honored by men. I tell you the truth, they have received their reward in full. But when you give to the needy, do not let your left hand know what your right hand is doing, so that your giving may be in secret. Then your Father, who sees what is done in secret, will reward you.

Giving to the needy is not the Christian mission. Preaching and sharing the gospel is. Making disciples is. Teaching others to fully obey Christ is.

Giving to the needy is what maturing, loving Christians come to do because it is what their role model, Jesus, did! If he did it, it is just the right thing to do. If Jesus did it, it is an important thing to do.

Why God allows human inequality, suffering, and poverty is a great and perplexing mystery of his nature and purpose. But he does allow it all. The reality is that God could fix it all in a moment. But he hasn't. At least, not yet. We cannot fix it all at once (and have not been able to in the eons of our existence). But he expects us to care and to try anyway. Jesus showed us. As

Paul says, he was reminded by those who originally walked with Jesus. They had told him, "we should continue to remember the poor" (Gal 2:10).

Jesus himself was poor in this world—"the Son of Man has no place to lay his head" (Luke 9:58). In fact, Jesus said that the poor are blessed (Luke 6:20). He said that being rich was a formidable obstacle to salvation (Luke 18:25). Being poor in this world is certainly not the worst thing that can happen to someone!

Jesus taught us to love one another. He said the whole law was summed up with two commands: loving God with our all and loving our neighbors as ourselves (Matt 22:37–40). He said we were to love one another with the same kind of love he has shown to us (John 13:34–35). In the famous parable of the Good Samaritan, Jesus showed that our "neighbor" is anyone, including a complete stranger, who has fallen on hard times and needs us (Luke 10:25–37).

Thus, Jesus did not say *if* you give to the needy. Jesus said *when* you give to the needy. See the difference? Not if, but when! How can we claim we are even trying to love like Jesus did and not show mercy to the needy?

Christians are the most generous people on the earth, for example, the Salvation Army, the Red Cross, etc. Let a tragedy happen, and see who shows up. Go to the poorest countries in the world and see who is there serving the needy. Look on the names of hospitals and orphanages and leper treatment centers and see who is behind so many of them.

But sadly, even with the great deeds of compassion and service Christ's people do collectively, it is still quite small compared to what *could* be done. So many Christians give little to nothing to the poor. Neither do they give as individuals to those they know or know about, nor through churches and organizations who serve the poor. What does that say about our faith? What does that say about the measure of our love? A verbal blessing to those who are hungry and cold without helping them is cold indeed. James said,

What good is it, my brothers and sisters, if someone claims to have faith but has no deeds? Can such faith save them? Suppose a brother or a sister is without clothes and daily food. If one of you says to them, "Go in peace; keep warm and well fed," but does nothing about their physical needs, what good is it? In the same way, faith by itself, if it is not accompanied by action, is dead. (James 2:14–17)

When we live like Jesus, it will be said of us, "When you give to the needy." Plain and simple.

Reflections:
1. Something to ask: Do I give to the poor? How much, proportionally, do I give to the poor? Do I give purposefully and generously to the poor? Do I inconvenience myself in order to give to the needy?
2. Something to think about: If I do not care about the needy, I do not care about Christ.
3. Something to believe: Jesus takes what we do for the least fortunate, both for good and bad, very personally.
4. Something to pray: Lord, open my heart, my life, and my resources to the needy.
5. Something to memorize: "But when you give to the needy, do not let your left hand know what your right hand is doing, so that your giving may be in secret" (Matt 6:3)
6. Something to do: Make a plan for giving regularly to the needy. One of the easiest things to do is to set up a regular contribution to a reputable charity so that you do not have to remember it (so that you do not forget to give). Try to grow your giving yearly.

26

Pray Like You Mean It

(Matt 6:5–8)

And when you pray, do not be like the hypocrites, for they love to pray standing in the synagogues and on the street corners to be seen by men. I tell you the truth, they have received their reward in full. But when you pray, go into your room, close the door and pray to your Father, who is unseen. Then your Father, who sees what is done in secret, will reward you. And when you pray, do not keep on babbling like pagans, for they think they will be heard because of their many words. Do not be like them, for your Father knows what you need before you ask him.

Probably nothing gives us more trouble than prayer. It really is the cutting edge of faith. Is God really there? Is he really listening? Does he really care about me? Am I, in all my sin, even getting through? It challenges us at the deepest levels concerning our beliefs about God, the world, and ourselves.

When we pray alone, we struggle to believe that our words get beyond the walls around us. When we pray aloud publicly, we are so intent on making sure we sound okay that we scarcely can think about speaking to God for fear of making a mistake, or worse yet, impressing or not impressing others. When we follow others in prayer, we get distracted and find our minds drifting far away to the trivial or even worse.

The reality is that our faith itself is work—God's work in us, and our work with God. "Then they asked him, 'What must we do to do the works God requires?' Jesus answered, 'The work of God is this: to believe in the one he has sent'" (John 6:28–29). The work God asks of us is for us to believe—to have faith in him. But it does take tremendous effort. Not so much effort with our physical bodies, but rather effort with our hearts and our minds and our souls. Prayer requires consistent thoughtfulness; prayer requires a growing faith; prayer requires planning; prayer requires mental discipline; and prayer requires self-control. Prayer requires us to trust in somebody and something unseen, rather than on ourselves, others, or anything seen.

It is odd that Jesus would call faith a work. But this is the work God requires of us. In fact, "Without faith it is impossible to please God, because anyone who comes to him must believe that he exists and that he rewards those who earnestly seek him" (Heb 11:6). The work in prayer is earnestly seeking him. Him. Prayer, when it is most connecting with God, is not self-centered, but God-centered. Our faith in prayer is not in our prayer-effectiveness, but is in God's goodness, grace, and concern for us.

"Your Father knows what you need before you ask him." Wow. Why should we ask, then? He knows everything about us, and about everybody else, for that matter. He even cares for us and for others infinitely more than we are capable of. And who am I to tell the Creator anything—what to do, what I need, or what others need? What is the point?

Prayer is connecting with God. You need to pray because you need to connect regularly with God. Prayer is like putting money into a savings account or investment, in some ways. When you hand over the cash or check, it disappears into the bank. If you are a smart investor, you try to forget about it unless you really, really need it. In actuality, your money is just a number stored on a computer disk somewhere. You cannot see it or touch it; you can only see a record of it somewhere. But it is there. Your prayer is heard and registered. The investment has been made with God. However, if prayer is for any other reason than to seek and connect with God, all bets are off. "Your Father, who sees what is done in secret, will reward you."

Prayer is similar in some ways to building and maintaining a marriage relationship. Husbands and wives develop this uncanny insight into each other, scarcely needing to talk to know what is going on with the other. Often they can communicate in "looks," grunts, groans, and facial expressions. But marriage needs constant reconnecting—another hug, another kiss, another "I love you." Intimacy requires constant reconnecting, even though what is being experienced has already been experienced many times before. Rehashing the old. Considering what is to come. Just connecting and staying connected.

My wife knows I need companionship, but it means tons to her for me to ask her to come sit by me. I know my wife loves me, but I always like hearing it again. I know my wife needs money allotted for things, but her reminders get or keep those things in the budget. I know my wife needs me to do certain things, but I need reminders at times amid everything else that demands my attention, and I also need her to help me know what the priorities are when I am making my plans.

God wants to hear from us. He is real, and he is personal—personable in fact. I do not have to understand everything about him to want to do something he asks for. I must trust him. And remember, something supernatural is going on when we pray.

The Spirit helps us in our weakness. We do not know what we ought to pray, but the Spirit himself intercedes for us with groans that words cannot express. And he who searches our hearts knows the mind of the Spirit, because the Spirit intercedes for the saints in accordance with God's will (Rom 8:26–27).

Prayer is supernatural because prayer involves the supranatural. It takes faith.

So pray. Just do it. "Let go, and let God…" Just start: "My Father in heaven…" Then talk to him. The Spirit will help you.

Reflections:
1. Something to ask: Why does God want, perhaps even need, us to pray?
2. Something to think about: What if God makes his work, and what he wants to do in and around us, contingent on our praying? What, then, is not happening in our lives that needs to, simply because we do not pray?
3. Something to believe: God works through our faith.
4. Something to pray: God, why do you care what I think, want, or believe needs to happen? Help me to believe.
5. Something to memorize: "When you pray, go into your room, close the door and pray to your Father, who is unseen" (Matt 6:6).
6. Something to do: Pray. Now.

27

Pray Like This

(Matt 6:9–15)

This, then, is how you should pray: "Our Father in heaven, hallowed be your name, your kingdom come, your will be done on earth as it is in heaven. Give us today our daily bread. Forgive us our debts, as we also have forgiven our debtors. And lead us not into temptation, but deliver us from the evil one." For if you forgive men when they sin against you, your heavenly Father will also forgive you. But if you do not forgive men their sins, your Father will not forgive your sins.

"Our Father in heaven, hallowed be your name." Perhaps some of the most often repeated words in the whole Bible. Hallowed means "regarded as holy." Holy means "set apart as sacred." God is wholly holy. Holy means "to be revered and worshiped." God is set apart because he *is* set apart. God is to be revered because he is worthy to be revered. And his very name should incite this realization. "You shall not misuse the name of the Lord your God, for the Lord will not hold anyone guiltless who misuses his name" (Exod 20:7). Hallowed be his name.

Prayer is at the cutting edge of worship. And worship aligns the universe rightly. God is the head of Christ; Christ is the head of humanity (1 Cor 11:3). But, in our own minds, we tend to get ahead of God, do we not? When my children were young, I remember going on trips and things. I remember how wherever we would go, the kids liked to get ahead of their mom and me. Sometimes *way* ahead. We constantly had to tell them to slow down and wait up. Why? Because there were potential perils ahead that we needed to protect them from. And they would most assuredly take wrong turns because they did not know where we were going. As youngsters, they could not read the maps and signs. They did not know their way. Plus, we wanted to be with them to experience things together. We wanted to be able to explain things so they could understand and get the full impact. Get it?

It is the same with us with God. We tend to get ahead of him and face perils on our own. We tend to forget he is even "back there." We tend to make wrong turns that lead us to wrong places. We lose sight of him and then end up crying out to him when we get lost. But, it is his voice we need to hear constantly:

He calls his sheep by name and leads them out. When he has brought out all his own, he goes on ahead of them, and his sheep follow him because they know his voice. But they will never follow a stranger; in fact, they will run away from him because they do not recognize a stranger's voice. (John 10:3–5)

Sheep follow the shepherd. They don't run ahead of their shepherd.

Do you remember being a kid and accidently pulling on the wrong woman's dress or pant leg, to the possible surprise of some lady who was not your mom? Do you possibly remember even grabbing the wrong leg, to the even greater shock of some woman who was not your mom? Well, prayer is grabbing the right leg. Prayer is tagging up. Prayer is getting back behind mom rather than in front of her.

"Your kingdom come, your will be done." May your total reign come soon, as we so desperately need it. "Give us our daily bread." And may we always be aware of where it all comes from. Forgive us our debts, our sins. We can accrue so many, so quickly!

And help us forgive others their sins as well, as it causes us all sorts of grief when we are unmerciful. We know your mercy is somehow contingent on ours. "And lead us not into temptation, but deliver us from the evil one." Help us not get ahead of you and get kidnapped by the ultimate counterfeit father—Satan.

Just start: "My Father in heaven…" You can take it from here…

Reflections:

1. Something to ask: What makes our prayers acceptable— helps them really connect—to our loving Father?
2. Something to think about: If God asks us to pray, there is a very good reason to pray!
3. Something to believe: God is waiting for and listens to our humble prayers.
4. Something to pray: Lord, teach us to pray.
5. Something to memorize: "Our Father in heaven, hallowed be your name, your kingdom come, your will be done on earth as it is in heaven. Give us today our daily bread. Forgive us our debts, as we also have forgiven our debtors. And lead us not into temptation, but deliver us from the evil one" (Matt 6:9–13).
6. Something to do: Sincerely pray this prayer throughout the day. Think about and savor each statement or request.

28

Make No Bones About It

(Matt 6:14–15)

For if you forgive men when they sin against you, your heav-
enly Father will also forgive you. But if you do not forgive
men their sins, your Father will not forgive your sins.

"For if you forgive men when they sin against you, your heavenly Father will also forgive you. But if you do not forgive men their sins, your Father will not forgive your sins." Read these words over and over. And then read them again. Tough words. But clear. Mercy is free, but it is not unconditional. There is indeed a difference between a price and a condition. God's forgiveness was earned at an awfully big price to Christ. It is not cheap. It is free to us, but it is not cheap to us either!

Many Christians seemingly have made Paul's letters the hub of the Bible. It is the tradition of a huge portion of Christ's church today. In this way of thinking, Jesus is reinterpreted through a way of looking at Romans. That is a mistake, I believe. Jesus—his personality, his perspective, his way of behaving—should be the hub of the whole Bible, not just the New Testament. The whole Old Testament plan was carried out and written down to get us to the conviction that "Jesus is Lord!" As we are told, "Christ is the culmination of the law…" (Rom 10:4). Thus, the Gospels should be the hub of the Bible because everything must be interpreted through the life and teaching of Christ. Anything else has lost connection with the Head, Christ (Col 2:19). Any alternative view, I believe, threatens to cheapen the grace and goodness of God. Only in knowing the power and awesomeness of God does grace fully shine. Jesus is the radiance of God's glory (Heb 1:3). He is a living lesson in theology, rather than simply an academic one.

So "let us be thankful, and so worship God acceptably with reverence and awe, for our God is a consuming fire" (Heb 12:28–29). A consuming fire! Do not mess with God.

Jesus gave a parable, recorded in Matthew 18:21–35, to drive home the point of God's conditional forgiveness. The story opens when Peter, getting that Jesus was upping the ante on forgiving others, asked him, "Lord, how many times shall I forgive my brother when he sins against me? Up to seven times?" Perhaps Peter tried to impress here. Not hardly, Jesus points out. "I tell you not seven times, but seventy-seven times." Some translations say seventy times seven. Either way, a lot.

The parable is about a king who was settling accounts with his servants. One guy owed the king the equivalent of several thousand dollars and was simply not able to pay. The king ordered him, his wife, his children, and all his possessions to be sold and the money paid on the debt. The guy begged, of course. "Be patient with me and I will pay back everything." The king canceled the debt!

Unbelievably, this guy went out and hunted down a fellow servant that owed him just a small amount. He grabbed the guy and began to choke him, demanding he repay the money! His fellow servant made the same request to him as the other had made to the king. However, unlike the merciful king, he refused to cancel the debt and had this man thrown into prison until he could repay the debt (kind of hard to do in prison, huh?).

Other servants went to the king and told him what this clown had done to the one that owed him just a few coins. Needless to say, the king was quite irate and called this unmerciful chap back in. He said, "You wicked servant, I canceled all that debt of yours because you begged me. Should you not have had mercy on your fellow servant just as I had on you?" His debt was reinstated (yes, God can reverse his own decisions, as he is sovereign!), and the unmerciful one was himself thrown into prison until he could repay his insurmountable debt!

Jesus concludes, "This is how my heavenly Father will treat each of you unless you forgive your brother from your heart." Jesus's death and resurrection did not change this. And even Paul makes it clear that God is sovereign in distributing his mercy: "I will have mercy on whom I have mercy, and I will have compassion on whom I have compassion" (Rom 9:14). So no matter how many times you have been "saved," you had better think twice about being unforgiving of others.

Peter was likely referring to the oral tradition of the Jews in asking about forgiving seven times. Peter probably thought that was a big number and that Jesus would be impressed. This was not the first time Jesus had taught forgiveness, of course. I doubt that Jesus was giving a specific number, as it is highly unlikely that another will sin specifically against us seven times, let alone seventy-seven—although our mates and children might technically reach those numbers with us, as we with them.

Jesus gave some specific instructions about reconciling to brothers that sin against us or are even angry with us for some reason. If you have something against a brother or are angry with one, you take responsibility and go to the brother and seek reconciliation, if necessary following up with a friend. Later, the matter may even need to be considered by the whole church (Matt 18:15–20). That is one of the discussions leading to the one just mentioned. And he had already said earlier that if you are coming to worship and remember your brother has something against you, you should first go straighten it out before you even bother to worship God (Matt 5:23). You take the initiative, either way!

So make no bones about it: God flat out expects you to be forgiving and merciful. "I desire mercy and not sacrifice" (Matt 9:13). As he told them, go and learn what this even means! We should, as well.

Reflections:
1. Something to ask: What should be the basis of our mercy toward others?
2. Something to think about: Why, when we are forgiven so much, is it so easy for us to be judgmental of and unmerciful to others (and, in fact, so difficult not to be)?
3. Something to believe: God's mercy toward us is conditional on our mercy toward others.
4. Something to pray: Help me, O Lord, to be merciful, as you are merciful, to the core of my being!
5. Something to memorize: "For if you forgive men when they sin against you, your heavenly Father will also forgive you. But if you do not forgive men their sins, your Father will not forgive your sins" (Matt 6:14–15).
6. Something to do: Make a list of those whom you feel have specifically sinned against you or whom you have something against. Go back as far as you can in your memory. Write down your particular beefs with them. Now, one by one and issue by issue, forgive them in prayer. Be very cognizant of how merciful God has been and is to you. Be that way toward them.

29

Go Fast

(Matt 6:16–18)

When you fast, do not look somber as the hypocrites do, for they dis-figure their faces to show men they are fasting. I tell you the truth, they have received their reward in full. But when you fast, put oil on your head and wash your face, so that it will not be obvious to men that you are fasting, but only to your Father, who is unseen; and your Father, who sees what is done in secret, will reward you.

Fasting baffles us, as do so many of the cultures and customs of Bible times. We love to eat. Eating is a great pleasure. Of course, we need to eat. God gave us the wonderful gift of taste to make it a pleasurable experience too. Eating is associated in some way with so many special events—Christmas, Thanksgiving, Easter, birthday parties, and more. Even God commanded certain feasts to be celebrated by the Jews. Two of the most important Judeo-Christian memorials, Passover and Eucharist, involve food. We even call some foods "comfort foods." That says a lot. No wonder, with our modern prosperity, there is such an epidemic of obesity!

But fasting has also been around through the centuries as well. And there's really quite a bit said about it in scripture. "When you fast": Jesus made an assumption, at least about his Jewish listeners, that they would indeed fast. "When" you fast…

Jesus fasted. In fact, Jesus fasted at the beginning of his ministry, during his forty-day testing in the wilderness (Matt 4:1–11). He also expected that his disciples would fast after he left—"then [after his departure from earth] they will fast" (Matt 9:14–15).

Only one fast was commanded in the Old Testament, and that was on the Day of Atonement. At least, it is assumed that fasting was a part of it. The phrase is translated different ways—"to deny yourself" or "to afflict your soul." But the meaning was for the fasters to stir themselves up on the inside. It was to intentionally deny themselves for a reason.

But fasting has no spiritual meaning if it has no proper spiritual purpose. It was never to be an empty ritual, and Jesus was making that point. One of Matthew's favorite prophets to quote, Isaiah, had a lot to say about the real purpose of fasting—repenting. He said it was to help those who were victims of injustice and oppression; to share with the hungry, the poor, and the homeless; and to not turn away from one's own family (Isa 58:3–9). Clearly, fasting was a time of remembering and cleansing and repenting. Perhaps it was and is a catharsis of sorts. However, in no way was it to be a ritual to be used for showing off one's righteousness and commitment.

"When you fast, do not look somber as the hypocrites do, for they disfigure their faces to show men they are fasting." If you do a thing to show off, that will be your only reward, if people are at all impressed in the first place. Rather, God would have us do it so that it "not be obvious to men that you are fasting, but only to your Father." As God sees in secret, he will reward and respond in secret.

Sometimes we must cleanse ourselves of this world—even of those things that are essential for living here, and that within themselves are not wrong, such as eating, so that we can connect fully with the "other" world. That is the dimension that is permanent and final. Sometimes we need to cease for a bit from doing only what our fleshly instincts tell us so that we can hear what the Spirit is telling us—so we can hear God (Gal 5:16–18).

Sometimes we need to demonstrate to ourselves and to God that we mean it and that we are serious about our relationships with him. We need to clear out all the clutter from our lives and for a bit remove every single thing that comes between him and us.

"When you fast": we need to "afflict our souls" to quicken them to the spiritual realities of injustice and poverty. "Blessed are those who mourn." Afflict your soul for God a bit sometimes. Go without food, or anything else you might choose, for a particular period. In this small act of self-denial, connect with the deeper spiritual realities and see what God might want you to see, think, say, or do. What might he want to do to you or for you or for someone else?

"When you fast," Jesus said. He assumed you would.

Reflections:
1. Something to ask: How much of the effect of our fasting should we expect to even see?
2. Something to think about: Why would Jesus assume that we fast when there is no specific command in the New Testament to do so?
3. Something to believe: Fasting matters.
4. Something to pray: God, teach me about fasting and lead me to fasts that are meaningful, helpful, and pleasing to you.
5. Something to memorize: "But when you fast, put oil on your head and wash your face, so that it will not be obvious to men that you are fasting, but only to your Father, who is unseen; and your Father, who sees what is done in secret, will reward you" (Matt 6:17–18).
6. Something to do: Fast. If you have never fasted, there are excellent books and articles on the subject. Before you fast, read one of these or talk to a trusted pastor or spiritual advisor about the subject.

30

Invest Wisely

(Matt 6:19–20)

Do not store up for yourselves treasures on earth, where moth and rust destroy, and where thieves break in and steal. But store up for yourselves treasures in heaven, where moth and rust do not destroy, and where thieves do not break in and steal.

Do not store treasures on earth. Rather, build up a big portfolio of stocks from heaven.

We invest in heaven with our minds, our hearts, our time, and our resources. The more we invest our possessions in the things of God, the more our hearts will be attached to spiritual things. The converse is true too, though. Invest it all here, and your heart will be here. "Set your hearts on things above, where Christ is seated at the right hand of God. Set your minds on things above, not on earthly things" (Col 3:1–2).

And it is not just about what we *do* either. It is as much about the motives for doing what we do. If I do "spiritual things" for worldly reasons, I will get only a worldly reward. Remember, "Be careful not to do your 'acts of righteousness' before men, to be seen by them. If you do you will have no reward from your Father in heaven" (Matt 6:1). Just be sure to invest in the right things for the *right* reason.

What we invest in is where we place our hope. It is where we find security. It is where we find a big part of identity, much like where we tell people we are from or what our family name is. Hoping in things of the world is disappointing—moths eat them, they rust, or they get stolen. Or we just get tired of those old things and are thus quickly off to acquire new ones.

But when we hope in that which is spiritual, we do not get disappointed (Rom 5:5). I have seen lots of broken hearts over things lost in this life—expensive things, inexpensive things, jobs, relationships, and dreams. It is sad, really. This is about people reaping what they have sown. No amount of counseling can reverse it. We can only help put it in a right perspective so they can move on and make better choices in the future.

Look at your bank statement. Look at your time planner. Take a look at the things you think about most of the time. You will see where your heart is. It always follows your investments.

If you want to be heavily invested in heavenly things, put your money where your mouth is, and your heart will end up there too!

Reflections:
1. Something to ask: What should our spiritual investment portfolios look like?
2. Something to think about: The value of our time is ultimately determined by what it was spent on.
3. Something to believe: Our return on investment in the spiritual is a hundredfold in this life!
4. Something to pray: Lord, may all I am and will ever be, be only for you.
5. Something to memorize: "But store up for yourselves treasures in heaven, where moth and rust do not destroy, and where thieves do not break in and steal" (Matt 6:20).
6. Something to do: Invest extravagantly in heaven today.

31

Values

(Matt 6:22–24)

The eye is the lamp of the body. If your eyes are good, your whole body will be full of light. But if your eyes are bad, your whole body will be full of darkness. If then the light within you is darkness, how great is that darkness! No one can serve two masters. Either he will hate the one and love the other, or he will be devoted to the one and despise the other. You cannot serve both God and Money.

When I was young, we sometimes played like we were looking for a buried treasure. We saw shows on television where they were doing that, and it inspired our play. Hunting an imaginary treasure and other such discovery games are fun for kids because, although they know the game is not real, there is still a thrill in it due to vivid imagination and the emotions it can stir.

I also remember watching game shows where people would win money and prizes. I even vaguely remember us sending in postcards to enter some sort of contest. We certainly did not have much, living out in the country. We were a family with just enough to get by. So thinking about having new cars and thousands of dollars and such was pretty exciting to me. Whatever I anticipated is what I thought about. A lot. Waiting to hear if we had won.

One time I invested in a small bag of silver. It cost about $500. A friend needed to sell it, and silver was hot at the time, so

I bought it from him. I had never paid any attention to the price of silver on the markets until then. I looked at it almost every day after that. Oh yeah, and I got to see it plummet to all-time lows! I deserved that, did I not?

Jesus summed it up pretty clearly. You *cannot* serve both God and money. Period. He did not say you could not *have* money. He did not say you did not need provisions to live life here and now. What he said was that you could not serve money and serve him at the same time.

What does it mean to serve money? Well, what we serve is what we live for (or whom we live for). Serving money is really about serving ourselves and serving others who can make life better for us. In the end, though, any idol I worship is ultimately "me, myself, and I!"

We do not fall into Satan's traps because we love him, worship him, and think he is awesome, as we do with Christ (although we can try to live selfishly for Christ too!). We serve Satan because we make a devil's pact with him to make life about "me." When we are serving Satan's purposes, it is because we are trying to serve self. But in this scenario, it is the devil that rules our lives. Satan offered temptation to Jesus in the wilderness: "All this I will give you if you will bow down and worship me" (Matt 4:9). Satan tried to make such a pact with Jesus for Jesus to worship him! Are you kidding me? No, Satan is real, and he is serious business. Jesus responded, "Away from me Satan! For it is written: 'Worship the Lord your God, and serve him *only*'" (Matt 4:10).

When we serve money, it is not about the money; it is the "me" in the deal. We have bought into temptation number three—follow Satan and "have it all." It's a lie, though. "The love of money is a root of all kinds of evil" (1 Tim 6:10). And again, "Keep your lives free from the love of money and be content with what you have" (Heb 13:5).

The lie is that I will actually find life in having things for myself. Just not true, though. "What good is it for a man to gain the whole world, and yet lose or forfeit his very self" (Luke 9:25)?

You are worth too much to let yourself be used by Satan. You were made for use by a king—for noble use!

"If anyone would come after me, he must deny himself and take up his cross daily and follow me. For whoever wants to save his life will lose it, but whoever loses his life for me will save it" (Luke 9:23–24). Deny self and "lose" your life in Christ. Then you will find real life. "Why spend money on what is not bread, and your labor on what does not satisfy" (Isa 55:2)? Ask yourself.

Putting all your marbles in this earthly basket is destining yourself for supreme disappointment—"there will be weeping and gnashing of teeth" (Matt 8:12). Do not dare set yourself up for the ultimate market crash in history for the world—the day Jesus returns—and find you have lost everything you invested in the temporal world. Do not fall for it. Yeah, it is tempting here, but it is infinitely *not* worth it. It is a scam. It is a ruse—of the greatest proportions!

Invest in heavenly things. Invest in God. Live for God every day. Do things that matter to him. Get up daily and do his bidding. Seek to make it your aim to please only him. You will find the ultimate life in doing that. And your heart will be with God, where it should be. He will give you life as only he can—to the full (John 10:10)!

Values are simply the things on which we put the greatest worth. Thus, value what is important—kingdom things. And serve the king only. The *only* king!

Reflections:
1. Something to ask: "Why spend money on what is not bread, and your labor on what does not satisfy"?
2. Something to think about: How can we tell if we are serving money or if we are using money to serve God?
3. Something to believe: You cannot live for God and live for the world.
4. Something to pray: Open my eyes, O God, to be ever aware of what my life is all about—whom I am serving.

5. Something to memorize: "No one can serve two masters. Either he will hate the one and love the other, or he will be devoted to the one and despise the other. You cannot serve both God and Money" (Matt 6:24).

6. Something to do: Evaluate what you think most about. Evaluate where you spend most of your time and money. Consider why you are spending your thoughts and your time and your money on certain things. Answer yes or no: are you serving God or money?

32

Anxiety Orders

(Matt 6:25-32)

Therefore I tell you, do not worry about your life, what you will eat or drink; or about your body, what you will wear. Is not life more important than food, and the body more important than clothes? Look at the birds of the air; they do not sow or reap or store away in barns, and yet your heavenly Father feeds them. Are you not much more valuable than they? Who of you by worrying can add a single hour to his life? And why do you worry about clothes? See how the lilies of the field grow. They do not labor or spin. Yet I tell you that not even Solomon in all his splendor was dressed like one of these. If that is how God clothes the grass of the field, which is here today and tomorrow is thrown into the fire, will he not much more clothe you, O you of little faith? So do not worry, saying, "What shall we eat?" or "What shall we drink?" or "What shall we wear?" For the pagans run after all these things, and your heavenly Father knows that you need them.

I do not think people are more anxious or depressed than they ever were. Not really. News reports continually mention the soaring rates of depression and anxiety disorders. I just think people are much more aware of them, and I think people report them more now and get treatment more often. After having counseled for nearly four decades, it seems clear to me, though, that in general people are indeed more neurotic these days.

Anxiety is an age-old issue. "Do not worry about your life." It is easier said than done, though.

Anxiety is our instinct. Anxiety is a form of fear. Fear is opposite of faith. To not worry is the opposite of our earthly instinct to survive, and thus it is our instinct to fear what threatens us. To not worry is what is not our instinct! But the Holy Spirit opposes our fleshly natures to keep us from being slaves to our mere animal instincts (Gal 5:17).

Someone once said that "life is what happens while you worry about the future." That is a very sad commentary on the existence of many of us, though. Precious time wasted.

But true faith saves us from such an existence. We begin to trust God to take care of us. We stop trying to play "god" in our own lives, in the lives of those we love, and in the world around us. When we try to play god, we end up trying to do what we cannot do, and instead not doing what we actually can. When the reality is in fact that God *can* do anything for us if he chooses—but he often does not. For Christ's own reasons, even one of the Apostle Paul's prayer requests were turned down (2 Cor 12:6–10). The fact is that "God" is a very stressful role for us to try to play. We too often unwittingly try to do it, though, and we wonder why we worry. This is the original lie—that we can "be like God"—that led to the original sin (Gen 3:5). But we really do know how weak and limited we are in the big scheme of things, do we not? But we try to control what we cannot control, and thus, we worry.

Look at the birds. Look at the flowering grasses. God nourishes and clothes them well. You know, I think most of us believe God will do that. I don't think most of our anxiety comes from not believing God will give us our daily needs—"Give us today our daily bread" (Matt 6:11). I believe what we mostly worry about is that God won't give us what we *want.* There's the rub.

True faith in God is the only antidote to humanity's anxiety—faith that God will direct us to the things we need and faith that God will deprive us of all that harms us too.

In my estimation, one of the most beautiful prayers ever written is called the "Serenity Prayer." It was written and published in the mid-twentieth century by Reinhold Niebuhr, a well-known professor, theologian, and philosopher. Alcoholics Anonymous made the first few lines of the prayer famous. Niebuhr rejected the utopianism of liberalism in favor of what is known as "Christian Realism." As opposed to an overemphasis on fixing the challenges of the world that we could do little about, his theology proposed an approach of acceptance and even embracing this world as it is, focusing on achieving the changes that are actually possible. I believe it embraces fully the philosophy of Jesus concerning worry and anxiety.

Serenity Prayer
God, grant me the serenity to accept the things I cannot change,
Courage to change the things I can, and the
wisdom to know the difference.
Living one day at a time; enjoying one moment at a time;
Accepting hardship as the pathway to peace.
Taking, as He did, this sinful world as it is, not as I would have it.
Trusting that He will make all things right if I surrender to His Will;
That I may be reasonably happy in this life,
And supremely happy with Him forever in the next. Amen.
(by Reinhold Niebuhr)

Let God be God, and you will see your anxiety level go way down. Faith is the antidote to anxiety. Trust, do not give sway to fear.

Reflections:
1. Something to ask: Why would a believer ever worry and be anxious about the things of this life?
2. Something to think about: Anxiety and its accompanying stress are at the root of much of human disease and discomfort. Thus, much healing is free.

3. Something to believe: God does not want us to be anxious. Period.

4. Something to pray: Lord, deliver me from anxiety. "I do believe; help me overcome my unbelief!" (Mark 9:24).

5. Something to memorize: "Therefore I tell you, do not worry about your life, what you will eat or drink; or about your body, what you will wear. Is not life more important than food, and the body more important than clothes?" (Matt 6:25).

6. Something to do: Talk to a spiritual advisor, mentor, counselor, or pastor if you are dealing with high anxiety. Otherwise, just confess ordinary anxieties to a peer or spiritual friend.

33

First Things First

(Matt 6:33–34)

But seek first his kingdom and his righteousness, and all these things will be given to you as well. Therefore do not worry about tomorrow, for tomorrow will worry about itself. Each day has enough trouble of its own.

Prioritization is one of our greatest challenges, if not *the* greatest. What should come first in our days, our years, or our lives? What should receive the most attention? What is important, and what is unimportant? What is just urgent but really not all that important? It can get really complicated. If we let it, that is.

A complicated life, for the Christian, is a corrupted life. Paul said, "But I fear, lest by any means, as the serpent beguiled Eve in his craftiness, your minds should be corrupted from the simplicity and the purity that is toward Christ"(2 Cor 11:3, American Standard Version). The simplicity. The New International Version translates this last phrase as "a pure and sincere devotion to Christ." But pure is simple, because *pure* means something is "only one thing."

Purity—the one thing—was what Mary chose over her harried sister Martha. "'Martha, Martha,' the Lord answered [Martha], 'you are worried and upset about many things, but few things are needed—or indeed only one. Mary has chosen what is better, and it will not be taken away from her'" (Luke 10:41–42). Only one thing is needed. Purity.

The way of Christ is quite simple. One thing. "Mary has chosen what is better, and it will not be taken away from her." She chose the one thing. We need to choose what is better. We need to choose what is best (Phil 1:9–10). However, as noted by many over the centuries, the unimportant often holds the important hostage.

When we truly put our faith in God, however, we accept that he will provide us with all that we need, and further, that he will keep from us that which we do not need. Hence, even hardships and deprivations are understood as blessings. "We know that in all things God works for the good of those who love him, who have been called according to his purpose" (Rom 8:28).

But again, too often we are most concerned about what we want rather than what we need. When that is so, we are still trying to "find our own lives" rather than losing our lives for Christ's sake (Luke 9:24). We have not come to completely trust him yet. We worry over tomorrow because we have not gotten today right yet. "Do not worry about tomorrow...[because] each day has enough trouble of its own."

What is it with you that contends with the kingdom priorities in your life? What are the weeds in your life that choke out his word—his kingdom (Matt 13:7)? What other "king" in your life rivals *the* king of the universe—Jesus Christ (Matt 28:18)? "If anyone comes to me and does not hate his father and mother, his wife and children, his brothers and sisters—yes, even his own life—he cannot be my disciple" (Luke 14:26). What should even rate on your charts compared to Jesus?

Far too many seek to make Jesus and "church" things only items on their priority charts. God first. Family second. Work third. And so on. This cannot be. Not for the disciple of Jesus. The king will not be compared to other things or individuals; neither will he be rivaled. He will, even perhaps impolitely, remove himself from such a priority list with his own form of "disappearing ink." He must own the list, or he will not truly even be on the list. Not in his mind, anyway—"I never knew you" (Matt 7:23), and, "The Lord knows those who are his" (2 Tim 2:19).

Every single item on my "to-do" list must be within his kingdom reign. If Jesus does not own your to-do list, he is not really even on it.

Jesus said, "Deny yourselves" (Luke 9:23) as if to say, "You must choose me over you." Because he chose you over himself (2 Cor 5:15). Jesus said, "any of you who does not give up everything…cannot be my disciple" (Luke 14:33).

If you get yourself aligned rightly with Jesus—if he reigns supreme in your life—everything else will align correctly. Worship does that for us. When I see Jesus as Lord, and when I worship and serve only him, all else falls into line. Or else falls off the chart altogether.

Reflections:
1. Something to ask: Is there anything in my life that rivals my devotion to Christ?
2. Something to think about: Anything that I truly own truly owns me.
3. Something to believe: If I seek and serve God faithfully, he will provide me what I really need, and he will deny me of what I really do not need.
4. Something to pray: O Lord, help me to seek first you and your kingdom.
5. Something to memorize: "But seek first his kingdom and his righteousness, and all these things will be given to you as well. Therefore do not worry about tomorrow, for tomorrow will worry about itself. Each day has enough trouble of its own" (Matt 6:33–34).
6. Something to do: Focus on today. Every time you catch yourself worrying about the future at all, bring your mind back to today. Pray for God's help.

34

The Judge Has Left the Building

(Matt 7:1–6)

Do not judge, or you too will be judged. For in the same way you judge others, you will be judged, and with the measure you use, it will be measured to you. Why do you look at the speck of sawdust in your brother's eye and pay no attention to the plank in your own eye? How can you say to your brother, "Let me take the speck out of your eye," when all the time there is a plank in your own eye? You hypocrite, first take the plank out of your own eye, and then you will see clearly to remove the speck from your brother's eye. Do not give dogs what is sacred; do not throw your pearls to pigs. If you do, they may trample them under their feet, and then turn and tear you to pieces.

I remember attending two Elvis Presley concerts back in the seventies. My wife had not actually been a fan prior to attending a concert, but after the first one, she was hooked. Her daddy loved her, spoiled her, and got her tickets. And not just to that first concert but another time as well! These concerts were grand events; Elvis was an incredible entertainer and wildly popular at the time. I cannot believe that some youngsters today do not even know who he was. Well, anyway, after one encore, the band would continue playing while cheers continued and then subsided. Then a booming voice would say, "Elvis has left the building." It was time for the adoring crowd to go home. Awed. Thrilled. A tad disappointed that it was over (at least for the girls).

For any of us to try to judge others would be like if I had tried to get on the stage and entertain after Elvis had left the building. Who would have wanted to listen? How silly and untalented would I have appeared? How could I have been more unqualified? The one who *could* judge us didn't come to judge. The one who is appointed as judge left. "I did not come to judge the world, but to save it" (John 12:47). The one who *is* qualified to judge will be back, though, to judge: "I will come back" (John 14:3).

Are we not just as silly when we try to seize the stage that Jesus has left? How could we be more unqualified? How much sillier can we look? And who cares what we think in such regard, anyway?

Yet we try. Trying to play Jesus's role is the same as when many of us sing our favorite singers' songs while we're in the shower. The echo effect even makes it begin to sound good to us. Right? Well, for the vast majority of us, it is probably a good idea that we not quit our day jobs. Trust me, it will not sound as good to others, and in fact, it would likely sound pretty bad—you know, like someone howling in the shower! Especially when they compare your singing to that of the performer you are imitating. In the same way, it looks and sounds just awful when we try to do Jesus's judging for him!

But we listen to ourselves pontificate on what is right and wrong and then we pronounce judgment on others, reading their minds and ascribing motives to their actions. We look down in indignation at the "sinners" around us. But remember that "man looks at the outward appearance, but the Lord looks at the heart" (1 Sam 16:7). That is all we have been given the *ability* to do—look at the outward appearance. We cannot read minds!

But Jesus "did not need man's testimony about man, for he knew what was in a man" (John 2:25). Jesus does read minds. "I the Lord search the heart and examine the mind, to reward each person according to their conduct, according to what their deeds deserve" (Jer 17:10). Jesus does not need us doing his work for him. We are simply not qualified. Or appointed. We have to look at appearance, and appearance can be very deceiving. He can see beyond appearance, and he is not to be deceived. About anything. "You Father...sees you in secret..." (Matt 6:6).

Each of us has a lens that is marked, perhaps marred, with our own knowledge and experiences. When we attribute to others' actions the motives that would be ours if we were to do such things, we make a huge mistake.

Let go of judgment, and let Jesus handle it. He has got it handled. You take care of your own business. Okay?

The Judge has left the building. For now. He will be back, however, to finish his work.

Reflections:
1. Something to ask: Why do we want to be the judges of others? What are our motives for being judgmental?
2. Something to think about: We will be judged by God, and other people, the same way we judge others. We should be kind and merciful.
3. Something to believe: There is in fact a kind of judgment (discernment, not condemnation) that God commands of us as his people in certain matters (1 Cor 2:15–16; 5:12–13). In this, the Holy Spirit leads us and qualifies us. There is a judgment of condemnation that we are absolutely not called to be involved in and are commanded not to be. We are not qualified for it in any way.
4. Something to pray: Dear God, forgive me of judging others. Help me to view others, and myself, in mercy. Help us to see others through your eyes. Help me to desire that others be shown mercy and be saved. Help me to err always on the side of mercy as I relate to others. Lead me to be merciful as you are merciful.
5. Something to memorize: "Do not judge, or you too will be judged. For in the same way you judge others, you will be

judged, and with the measure you use, it will be measured to you" (Matt 7:1–2).

6. Something to do: Evaluate the lens through which you typically look at others. Is that lens critical and condemning? Or is it the lens that gently lightens others' dark spots, so to speak, and makes their sins fade out of the picture? Remember, God sees Christians as "holy and blameless in his sight."

35

Just Ask

(Matt 7:7–11)

Ask and it will be given to you; seek and you will find; knock and the door will be opened to you. For everyone who asks receives; he who seeks finds; and to him who knocks, the door will be opened. Which of you, if his son asks for bread, will give him a stone? Or if he asks for a fish, will give him a snake? If you, then, though you are evil, know how to give good gifts to your children, how much more will your Father in heaven give good gifts to those who ask him!

Just ask. Really? "Ask, and you will receive." This sounds too good to be true, and we all know that if something sounds too good to be true, it usually is not true. What can this literally mean?

When company comes, the hospitable host will often say something like, "make yourself at home, and if you need anything, just ask." Just ask. That is love and hospitality speaking. When we say it, do we mean that if a guest asks for a pink elephant that we will get it for him or her, no matter what? Or if a guest asks for heroin that we will run and get some? No, we are making a loving, hospitable statement that requires just a touch of understanding and discernment. We are being hospitable.

And for sure, God is hospitable. He wanted you born, and he wants you born again into his kingdom. God takes care of and treats well even those people that do not love and serve him—"He causes his sun to rise on the evil and the good" (Matt 5:45). God is a great host—as if saying, "Make yourself at home; ask for anything you need."

However, consider this: "You do not have, because you do not ask God. When you ask, you do not receive, because you ask with wrong motives, that you may spend what you get on your pleasures" (James 4:2–3). So are there indeed some qualifications placed on Jesus's promises? Of course.

Have you ever asked God for something and not received it? Have you been seeking to know something and still don't have an answer? Have you been, "knock, knock, knockin' on heaven's door" as the old Bob Dylan song said, but feel unanswered at times (or even mostly)?

Well, Jesus's statements, as with our statements of hospitality, are clearly truisms, principles, or generalizations and not absolute promises in the strictest sense. "How much more will your Father in heaven give good gifts to those who ask him?" God will indeed give you good gifts. He is not going to give you bad gifts, though. God is not going to give you something you do not need at all—good or bad—or give you something you might otherwise need but at a time when you do not need it. We may acquire it in a human way, apart from God. Or we may acquire such in an evil way. But God will not be the giver.

We can knowingly or unknowingly ask for things that are actually bad for us. "When you ask, you do not receive, because you ask with wrong motives that you may spend what you get on your pleasures" (James 4:3). Or, "If anyone sees his brother commit a sin that does not lead to death, he should pray and God will give him life. I refer to those whose sin does not lead to death. There is a sin that leads to death. I am not saying that he should pray about that" (1 John 5:16). Hmmm. There's something we should *not* ask for, huh?

We also know God is not going to listen up much if we ask for things that contradict his will and purpose—"This is the confidence we have in approaching God: that if we ask anything according to his will, he hears us" (1 John 5:14). According to *his* will. Yes, indeed, he has a purpose in this world—*his* world—and, more specifically, a purpose in each of our lives. He is not going to give us things that ultimately counter his purposes.

A loving parent does not give a twelve-year-old a car to drive. Or a car he requests for his eleven-year-old friend to drive! A loving parent does not give his four-year-old a loaded gun to play with. No matter how many times the child asks. Clearly, neither does God do such—"how much more will your Father in heaven give good gifts to those who ask him." You may indeed get something harmful for yourself. But God will not be the one that gives it to you. Satan: "All this I will give you" (Matt 4:9). Yeah, Satan can apparently give gifts too!

However, remember: "Don't be deceived, my dear brothers. Every good and perfect gift is from above, coming down from the Father of the heavenly lights, who does not change like shifting shadows" (James 1:16–17). That last sentence is important too. God does not change on us. He is very consistent.

A friend told me one time that his dad had, throughout his life, made all these statements about what he was going to do for him as his son. However, after he had made the statements, he often never even brought them back up again, let alone actually do much of what he had promised. I could see on my friend's face and hear in his voice the disappointment still from those dashed expectations, even though he was sure his dad was only thinking out loud at those times and had just changed his mind. His dad was, like the rest of us, a fallen human. God is not that, however.

God does not change his mind that way. And he does not forget. "The Lord is not slow in keeping his promise, as some understand slowness. He is patient with you, not wanting anyone to perish, but everyone to come to repentance" (2 Pet 3:9). However, remember that God's time perspective is quite different from ours—"With the Lord a day is like a thousand years and a thousand years are like a day" (2 Pet 3:8). His timing might not be what we want. But his timing is also perfect. Our timing is not. Patience is required when working with God.

So ask for the things you think are good and right. "By prayer and petition, with thanksgiving, present your requests to God" (Phil 4:6). Know that he hears. Know he will surely answer. And, know he hears the real prayer—the prayer of your heart that *you* may not really even get—"The Spirit helps us in our weakness. We do not know what we ought to pray, but the Spirit himself intercedes for us with groans that words cannot express" (Rom 8:26).

Ask. Seek. Knock. Trust. Good things will come.

While you are here, if you need anything at all, just ask.

Reflections:

1. Something to ask: How can we know how to ask according to God's will?

2. Something to think about: How do we know our blessings are from God and not just a matter of happenstance or luck?

3. Something to believe: All good gifts come from God! (James 1:17)

4. Something to pray: Lord, I pray for wisdom, not riches. I pray for strength, not relief. I pray for others to receive gifts today that I might otherwise have received. I pray in your infinite wisdom that you give me only the good gifts that I will use to your glory and never what I might misuse to the harm of myself or others.

5. Something to memorize: "Ask and it will be given to you; seek and you will find; knock and the door will be opened to you. For everyone who asks receives; he who seeks finds; and to him who knocks, the door will be opened" (Matt 7:7–8).

6. Something to do: Make a prayer list of the things you wish for that you believe are according to his will. Keep it handy and pray from it.

36

The Golden Rule

(Matt 7:12)

*So in everything, do to others what you would have them do
to you, for this sums up the Law and the Prophets.*

There is perhaps not a more quoted verse of scripture than this:
"In everything, do to others what you would have them do to
you." Many learned it first from the King James Version of the
Bible—"Do unto others, as you would have them do unto you." I
know that language does not resonate with those who have had
access to more modern English translations, but for those of us
who heard it as youngsters, that is the way we automatically think
it. Right?

Why does this command of Jesus resonate so well with most
of us? Well, perhaps because it is simple and clear, and it is a
summary of a lot of scripture—"this sums up the Law and the
Prophets"—the whole Old Testament, really. It is said by those
who spend their time counting them, that there are over six
hundred laws in the Law of Moses, so it is pretty hard to remember them all. This rule sums it up nicely, though. The Golden
Rule is always a good stab at what is best, even though what we
might wish others to do for us might turn out to be unwise or
even sinful. But indeed most of generally wish for similar kinds
treatment.

Sadly, a second reason it resonates even with those who are not believers in Christ is that it is self-referential. We humans can be very selfish, so it's easy to think about "what you would have them do to you." But it is really another way of saying, "Love your neighbor as yourself" (Matt 22:39).

However, the problem for us is in the application of the "self" part. We do not love ourselves very much a lot of the time, do we? At least, we do not treat ourselves too well. And some of the things we would have others do to us are not always in our own best interests. Right?

But Jesus's original audience for these words was the Jews. And the Law of Moses was their law, read regularly at the synagogues they attended.

Actually, Jesus later amends his love command for his disciples—"As I have loved you, so you must love one another" (John 13:34). In Jesus's new way, Jesus is the reference point, not us. I do not have to figure out how to treat others in specific situations based on what I would want. Rather, I only have to look for what Jesus would want me to do to or for them.

The Apostle Paul got this. In his instructions to the Ephesian Christians of the first century concerning relationships, he laid the foundation with, "Submit to one another out of reverence for Christ" (Eph 5:21). See, we decide how to treat people by referring to our reverence for Christ, not by their "deserving-ness" or lack thereof.

Again, "Wives, submit to your husbands as to the Lord" (Eph 5:22). Note the "as to the Lord," again referring the treatment back to Christ's way. And, "Husbands, love your wives, just as Christ loved the church and gave himself up for her" (Eph 5:25). And, by the way, when you look at this passage that is often so deeply resented by those seeking to improve women's lots, the whole meaning changes to something very positive for women. Christ does not lead by domination, and he does not require forced labor. Subjugation was and is a part of the curse—"he will rule over you" (Gen 3:16). Ruling over others is the way sinful people lead and control. In fact, it was Christ who submitted most, coming as a lowly servant. We serve a "meek and lowly" God (Matt 11:29, King James Version), not a "high and mighty one." And, that is how he requires all his leaders to lead, including husbands—"The rulers of the Gentiles lord it over them... not so with you" (Matt 20:25).

"Children, obey your parents in the Lord" (Eph 6:1). "Fathers, do not exasperate your children; instead, bring them up in the training and instruction of the Lord" (Eph 6:4). Even parents who must guide and discipline their children are to nurture them, not simply dominate them, wearing them out with rules and unrealistic expectations.

Get it? Refer all your behaviors to Christ's. For the disciple, that is indeed what we would have others do to us. How we want to be treated is how Christ would want us treated. How we want to treat others is how Christ would have us treat them.

"So we make it our goal to please him" (2 Cor 5:9) and not ourselves. Please him. That is our aim. Not to please us. As disciples, we can read it this way: "In everything, do to others what Christ would do to or for them in the same circumstance. For this sums up his Sermon on the Mount!"

"Follow God's example, therefore, as dearly loved children and walk in the way of love, just as Christ loved us and gave himself up for us as a fragrant offering and sacrifice to God" (Eph 5:1–2).

Reflections:

1. Something to ask: How can the whole Law and Prophets be summed up so simply?
2. Something to think about: If the Law, concerning our treatment of others, was summed up by this rule as well as by Christ's command to love your neighbor as yourself, why did Christ give a new command (John 13:34–35)?
3. Something to believe: When we strive to live and love as Christ did, we will always come closest to doing what is true and right.

4. Something to pray: Lord, lead me to see and treat others as you do.

5. Something to memorize: "So in everything, do to others what you would have them do to you, for this sums up the Law and the Prophets" (Matt 7:12).

6. Something to do: Go do something very kind and generous for someone who definitely does not "deserve" it. Do it secretly and expect nothing from anybody else. Do not even hint to anyone else of what you have done.

37

You Be Careful Now

(Matt 7:13–14)

Enter through the narrow gate. For wide is the gate and broad is the road that leads to destruction, and many enter through it. But small is the gate and narrow the road that leads to life, and only a few find it.

Often, when those we love have to go somewhere, as they are getting ready to drive off, we will say something to the effect of, "You be careful." We usually already know they know they should. But we also know there are perils in the world, and we tend to get hurt by them when we are not being watchful and thoughtful. We can get careless, can we not? No texting while driving! Definitely no drinking and driving!

Sadly, we tend to get most careless with those things, activities, and people with which or with whom we are most familiar—mates, children, parents, good friends, and so on. And God! "In him we live and move and have our being" (Acts 17:28). That is pretty familiar, huh? He has just always been there.

And the more perilous a course is, the more careful we must be. "Small is the gate and narrow the road that leads to life." It is not that God is trying to make the path difficult. It is just that God is so great. And God is so perfect. And he *is* the way—"I am the *way* and the truth and the life" (John 14:6).

Sin literally means "missing the mark" (Greek, *hamartia*). Of course, even with our best efforts, because of our fallen nature, we miss the mark of God's perfection—"All have sinned and fall short of the glory of God" (Rom 3:23). We shoot our hardest and straightest at being just like him. That must be the goal of each of us, every day! But we fall short, even when we give it our best shot! The goal is fixed. It is not a moving target—"Be perfect, therefore, as your heavenly Father is perfect" (Matt 5:48).

No coach or teacher expects a performer to be perfect. Right? Each realizes no one can be. But the great teachers expect us to *try* to be perfect. An old Chinese proverb I heard somewhere many years ago says: "I'd rather shoot at the sky and hit a tree than shoot at a tree and hit a rock." Our goal *is* God—his likeness and nature. He calls us to his very own excellence. "His divine power has granted to us all things that pertain to life and godliness, through the knowledge of him who called us to his own glory and excellence" (2 Pet 1:3, Revised Standard Version). We are called to his very own excellence! He does this so that we can actually "participate" in his divine nature—to be more and more like him (2 Pet 1:4). The whole Creation itself is designed to declare God's divine nature (Rom 1:20).

So the way to life is narrow and thus perilous, because the way *is* God. The way is to be like God. In our fallen condition, the forces against our doing so are tremendous. "For our struggle is not against flesh and blood, but against the rulers, against the authorities, against the powers of this dark world and against the spiritual forces of evil in the heavenly realms" (Eph 6:12). And thus, "I delight in God's law; but I see another law at work in the members of my body, waging war against the law of my mind and making me a prisoner of the law of sin at work within my members" (Rom 7:22–23).

Our default mode is the broad way though. It is easy. It is instinct. On it, we do not have to be thoughtful of others unless it is of benefit to us. We do not have to be careful other than in protecting our own interests. We can live as carelessly as we want. Living that way is often is just more "fun" and pleasurable.

But it is a steep, one-way, downhill, ice-covered, well-worn, and smoothly paved road into a brick wall. And on it, we have lots of company too—"many enter through it." However, it still leads directly to destruction. Once you are on the broad road, it can be very hard to make a U-turn, let alone just stop and pull over. It is best not to ever get on it. But when you do (and you will at some point), get off as soon as you realize where you are headed. God is indeed there to help you. He is on your side every time.

So be sure to go through the right gate, and you will be on the right road. Then, take care every day to line yourself up straight toward God so you will be sure to *stay* on the right road. Just remember, it is always the narrow one with the small gate. Oh, yeah, and sadly, although it is narrow, it will not be very crowded.

So you be careful. You hear?

Reflections:
1. Something to ask: What is so hard about the Christian way?
2. Something to think about: Can one think one is on the right road but be on the wrong one (2 Cor 13:5)?
3. Something to believe: If we truly seek God from the heart, and if we are truly honest, God won't let us stay on a wrong course.
4. Something to pray: Lord, lead me down the right road—the road to you!
5. Something to memorize: "Enter through the narrow gate. For wide is the gate and broad is the road that leads to destruction, and many enter through it. But small is the gate and narrow the road that leads to life, and only a few find it" (Matt 7:13–14).
6. Something to do: Visualize yourself going through a very narrow gate, holding onto Jesus himself. Picture a

walk only two bricks wide. Sense the challenge. Sense the need for care and balance. Sense the need to hold on to the steady strength of Jesus. Now, go do that for real today.

38

The Scary Reality of Counterfeit Christianity

(Matt 7:15–20)

Watch out for false prophets. They come to you in sheep's clothing, but inwardly they are ferocious wolves. By their fruit you will recognize them. Do people pick grapes from thornbushes, or figs from thistles? Likewise every good tree bears good fruit, but a bad tree bears bad fruit. A good tree cannot bear bad fruit, and a bad tree cannot bear good fruit. Every tree that does not bear good fruit is cut down and thrown into the fire. Thus, by their fruit you will recognize them.

They are often called "knockoffs": goods that are made to look like the real thing. They will have the brand names and logos of the real thing—the much more expensive, original version. They are illegal too.

The average person often cannot tell the difference between a knockoff and an original. Only those that deal in the originals can be sure which is a knockoff. There are indeed distinguishing characteristics, usually hidden from the untrained eye. The most obvious difference is who actually makes them. Counterfeiters make the fakes even though they put the designer's label on them.

Knockoffs are not made by the right factory. They are certainly not of the same quality in materials or workmanship. That's why they are cheaper—too good a deal to be true. However, they are in fact deals that are "too bad to be true." Because they are not true.

God makes us the real deal—true Christians. Only he can! "We are God's workmanship" (Eph 2:10). Following Jesus makes us true disciples of him. Simply Christian.

But Satan is a counterfeiter. He wants us to be his, and he makes us cheap. He is as a pimp who makes us his prostitutes. "Bow down and worship me" (Matt 4:9). His first effort is to keep us from even knowing about Jesus. His second is to keep us from knowing Jesus as Lord and Savior. His third strategy is to make us knockoffs and not the real thing—just counterfeits. He does it by deceiving us. Smoke. Mirrors. Darkness. Distraction. Deception. "Anything goes" with Satan.

"I am afraid that just as Eve was deceived by the serpent's cunning, your minds may somehow be led astray from your sincere and pure devotion to Christ" (2 Cor 11:3). Satan tries to trip us and knock us off the narrow way of God.

And he uses deception because he is the ultimate deceiver. He uses deceivers among us too. "Such men are false apostles, deceitful workmen, masquerading as apostles of Christ. And no wonder, for Satan himself masquerades as an angel of light. It is not surprising, then, if his servants masquerade as servants of righteousness" (2 Cor 11:13–15). Satan is a counterfeit and a counterfeiter.

"Watch out for false prophets. They come to you in sheep's clothing." As if to say they wear wool suits, do you think? They look like the real thing—preachers of God. They are not. They are knockoffs. And there are horns and sharp teeth hidden beneath all the wool. Deception. They may be deceived themselves. About themselves. Certainly about God. And so they are about others too.

You can recognize them by their fruit, but that fruit is not the obvious thing most people look for. The point is that it is *not* obvious. In our modern world—in modern Christianity—"nice" is the operative description expected of leaders of God. Friendly. Pleasing. Pleasant. Unoffensive.

But Jesus was, for the most part, not that way at all! In fact, Jesus was the stone people would stumble over. "See, I lay in Zion a stone that causes men to stumble and a rock that makes them fall, and the one who trusts in him will never be put to shame" (Rom 9:23). Jesus is the stone people stumble over. They trip over him because they find him offensive. He is not the way they want him to be. Jesus: "If the world hates you, keep in mind that it hated me first" (John 15:18). But false prophets must be liked. False prophets must be popular. False prophets must keep their "jobs" safe—safe with the people that gather them, train them, and pay them. Even seemingly adore them—worship them. "Woe to you when everyone speaks well of you, for that is how their ancestors treated the false prophets" (Luke 6:26). On the other hand, most of the original genuine prophets of God were killed. Jesus, our ultimate model, was killed. Butchered, really.

Paul warned it would happen—"For the time will come when men will not put up with sound doctrine. Instead, to suit their own desires, they will gather around them a great number of teachers to say what their itching ears want to hear" (2 Tim 4:3). That warning came nearly two thousand years ago. We can suppose then it has happened by now, I guess. By training men and women in "our" colleges to teach "our" churches "our" beliefs, if we are not very careful, we will all then be properly "branded" with the original designer's label, but produced in our own factories, not his. Denominated. "Named." Possibly even branded by the counterfeiters rather than by Christ. Knockoffs.

John: "We know that we have come to know him if we obey his [Jesus's] commands. The man who says, 'I know him,' but does not do what he commands is a liar, and the truth is not in him" (1 John 2:3–4). Not because we go to the right church. Not because we have all the right "deeper doctrines." But that we obey what Jesus says, that is what is all-important. We must obey *his* commands, not *theirs*.

False prophets lead you to them. Authentic ones lead you to him. And not just in name only.

Reflections:

1. Something to ask: What do you need to do, learn, or grow in so that you can differentiate the genuine things of God from the counterfeit imitations?

2. Something to think about: Being "very Christian" does not necessarily make one very Christian.

3. Something to believe: Jesus will save us from counterfeit Christianity if we let him. But it is a decision that we must make daily (Luke 9:23).

4. Something to pray: Lord, help me to be genuine and to be able to distinguish the real from the counterfeit.

5. Something to memorize: "Watch out for false prophets. They come to you in sheep's clothing, but inwardly they are ferocious wolves" (Matt 7:15).

6. Something to do: Pray today that God gives you the spiritual vision to recognize the authentic, so that you can differentiate it from the counterfeit. Pray that you can learn to do this without being overly suspicious or, worse yet, judgmental. It is not easy. But the way has a narrow gate and a straight, narrow road.

39

The Test of Authenticity

(Matt 7:21–23)

Not everyone who says to me, "Lord, Lord," will enter the kingdom of heaven, but only he who does the will of my Father who is in heaven. Many will say to me on that day, "Lord, Lord, did we not prophesy in your name, and in your name drive out demons and perform many miracles?" Then I will tell them plainly, "I never knew you. Away from me, you evildoers!"

The fruit to look for so you know who the counterfeiters are is the counterfeit Christian crop they produce. These are Christians who call Jesus Lord but who do not do the will of the Father. The will of God is that we grow in the character of Christ as revealed in the very lessons Jesus has been teaching us on the mountain. Counterfeit Christians may prophesy with power, drive out demons, and even perform amazing miracles. But still, Jesus pronounces them "knockoffs." They are "evildoers!" "I never knew you," he will say on that final day. Scary.

Good fruit? "Only he who does the will of my Father who is in heaven." It is not about religion. That can be faked. It is not about rites and rituals. They can be meaningless and even made-up. It is not about great preaching, great power, or great evangelism. Those too can be faked and done for wrong motives. It is certainly not about being the "nicest" or the most popular. It is about doing the will of our only true Father. His time on the mountain with you—his Sermon on the Mount—is meant to reveal to you what *his* real will is. And it is first really all about your character. It is about who he really wants you to *be*, not just about what he wants you to *do*. "First clean the inside of the cup and dish" (Matt 23:26).

Bad fruit? Counterfeiters producing counterfeits. And there are, in Jesus's own estimation, plenty of takers. "Many will say to me on that day…"

So let the buyer beware. "A bad tree cannot bear good fruit." To know if it is a knockoff, check to see what tree it came from. Who grew it? Who made it? Does it lead you to him (Jesus), or does it lead to them (the false prophets)? Are they leading you to Jesus? Or are they leading you to themselves? Are they stamping a human brand on you? A human name on you? Anything other than Jesus, simply Jesus? Simply Christian?

Either way, Jesus says we are responsible for differentiating. Watch out! We each are qualified to do that if we simply listen to him and do what he has given us the right and the ability to do—"his sheep follow him because they know his voice. But they will never follow a stranger; in fact, they will run away from him because they do not recognize a stranger's voice" (John 10:4–5).

And it is our fates that lie in the balance. Run from the counterfeiters. Faithfully listen to and follow only the Good Shepherd and those who lead you to him.

Reflections:

1. Something to ask: Are you tuned in to Jesus in such a way that you can recognize the counterfeit?

2. Something to think about: If you want to, you can trust in people to assure your salvation and rightness with God. It is very unwise, though. There is no real assurance in it. And those that are the most insistent that they solely are the right ones probably are not. Humility is one of the first marks of authenticity when it comes to Jesus.

3. Something to believe: Holding to Jesus's teaching assures your authenticity (John 8:31; 1 John 2:3-6; Ja 1:22-24).

4. Something to pray: Show me yourself, O Lord, that I may hear and know your will and not be deceived by false prophets—counterfeiters.

5. Something to memorize: "Not everyone who says to me, 'Lord, Lord,' will enter the kingdom of heaven, but only he who does the will of my Father who is in heaven" (Matt 7:21).

6. Something to do: Review the Sermon on the Mount, Matt 5–7. Look at the different parts and things you have been reading. Based on Jesus's teachings here, what do you think we must be about so we can "do the will of my our Father in heaven"?

40

The Wise Man Built His House upon the Rock

(Matt 7:24–27)

Therefore everyone who hears these words of mine and puts them into practice is like a wise man who built his house on the rock. The rain came down, the streams rose, and the winds blew and beat against that house; yet it did not fall, because it had its foundation on the rock. But everyone who hears these words of mine and does not put them into practice is like a foolish man who built his house on sand. The rain came down, the streams rose, and the winds blew and beat against that house, and it fell with a great crash.

Many who attended Sunday school as children sang about these verses: *The wise man built his house upon the rock. The wise man built his house upon the rock. The wise man built his house upon the rock, and the rains came tumbling down.* I wonder if we have yet grasped what it means, though.

"Everyone who hears these words of mine and puts them into practice is like a wise man who built his house on the rock." Jesus was using a parable here that would have made sense to local listeners. Some nomadic people would build out on the sands of the flood plains. It was quick, easy, and it was flat. The water kept the area pretty clean. Even of nomadic camps.

These were desert washes, and when the water rose, the whole community would be quickly swept away as the sand washed from under them. They were likely used to it though, even if they were disappointed when it happened (probably not for the first time either).

More stable communities built their houses on higher ground. They took the time to dig the sand out and set their foundations on the bedrock beneath. Even when the inevitable storms came, although damage might be sustained, the house would stand, ensuring the safety of the inhabitants and their possessions. They also would still have a place to live.

Hearing the voice of Jesus requires clarity of purpose, resolve, and focus. He will not generally yell. He will not compete with the din we allow into our lives. He will not force himself on us. So you'd better get to know his voice. Get to know his channel and lock your dial onto it. Do not allow anyone else to control your remote. And no channel surfing. Stay tuned!

Hearing and obeying only the voice of Jesus requires us to dig away any "sand" that is between him and us. Hearing and obeying the voice of Jesus requires that we fix our foundation squarely and firmly on him, "the Rock of Ages."

On the mountain, we see God. The light is bright. The sky is blue. The air is clean. We are above it all. Even mostly above any storm clouds. Nothing between him and us. Nothing obscures us from his glory there—"The heavens declare the glory of God; the skies proclaim the work of his hands" (Ps 19:1).

In the valley, there are shadows and obstacles that can shroud him from us. There are shadows and the early darkness. Creatures lurk in the shadows. We can get lost all too easily. We can fall going down. We must learn to recognize his kind, gentle, guiding voice. The Shepherd. My Shepherd. Thus, "I will fear no evil."

Another well-known passage: "The Lord is my shepherd, I shall lack nothing...Even though I walk through the valley of the shadow of death, I will fear no evil, for you are with me; your rod and your staff, they comfort me" (Ps 23:1, 4). He is there. He is not silent. But he only invites; he does not force. Not now, anyway. And he protects. We can live in faith rather than fear. Security rather than worry. Faith is the antidote to fear.

We do have to go down off the mountain, you know. We have to live in the world just now. God sends us there. But he prays for our safety. Jesus: "My prayer is not that you take them out of the world but that you protect them from the evil one. They are not of the world, even as I am not of it" (John 17:15–16). He goes down with us—"I will be with you always..." (Matt 28:20).

We have to live in this world just now, even though an experience with Christ will make you often want to just go on home—"For to me, to live is Christ and to die is gain" (Phil 1:21). But safety here is only on the Rock, not on the sands. It takes effort to build on the rock, though. It takes effort and elbow grease. "The work of God [the work God wants us to do; see verse 28] is this: to believe in the one he has sent" (John 6:29). It takes "want-to." It takes digging deeply, sometimes through rocky soil and other debris.

The house on the rock? "It did not fall, because it had its foundation on the rock." Good news.

The house on the sand? "It fell with a great crash." The song: "And the foolish man's house went *splat*!" Tragic. So sad. Bad news.

Maybe you know the song:

The wise man built his house upon the rock. (Repeat three times.) *And the rains came tumbling down. The rains came down and the floods came up.* (Repeat three times.) *And the wise man's house stood firm.*

But the foolish man built his house upon the sand. (Sing three times.) *And the rains came tumbling down.* (Sing three times.) *And the foolish man's house went* splat!

So, build your house on the Lord Jesus Christ. (Sing three times.) *And the blessings will come down!*

The blessings will come down from him. You know it, do you not?

The Rock on which you sit upon the mountain of God is the same bedrock beneath the surface in the valley. Remember its strength and security. Remember how it feels. Even in the dark night in the valley of the world, dig down to it to rest. Anchor yourself to it. Even when the storms come, although they beat on you, you will not wash away.

And you will walk another day to go back upon the mountain of God. With God. And then, one day, you will not have to come down. Ever again. And it will all be worth it. It will all make sense.

But for now, you must trust Christ. Trust and obey. Simple. Hard. But doable. He is so full of love and grace. "I have come that they might have life, and have it to the full" (John 10:10). Life here with the Shepherd? Good. Eternal life with him later? Unbelievable, incredible, "out of this world!"

Take the time to do it right. Build your house on the Rock.

Reflections:
1. Something to ask: What does digging down to build on the Rock, Christ, look like in real life?
2. Something to think about: Many times, the hurts and tragedies that people face and end up in counseling over are simply the result of careless building. When the storms come, what they have built is washed away. The cost can be so tragic, costly, and devastating.
3. Something to believe: Built on Christ, your house will never wash away. Period.
4. Something to pray: Lord, help me build my house on the rock that is you. May my anchor to you be secure.
5. Something to memorize: "Therefore everyone who hears these words of mine and puts them into practice is like a wise man who built his house on the rock" (Matt 7:24).

6. Something to do: Visualize digging deeply under yourself toward the bedrock of Christ. As a foundation company might go in under a foundation and pour concrete piers down to the bedrock, picture yourself doing that even now in your own spiritual foundation.

Conclusion:

Coming Down off the Mountain

(Matt 7:28–29)

When Jesus had finished saying these things, the crowds
were amazed at his teaching, because he taught as one who
had authority, and not as their teachers of the law.

"When Jesus had finished saying these things, the crowds were amazed at his teaching." Jesus is amazing. Jesus's teaching is amazing. Jesus's life is amazing. Jesus's love is amazing.

"He taught as one who had authority." He had authority, so he spoke that way. Others had not had the authority to say much of what they said. "My teaching is not my own. It comes from Him who sent me" (John 7:16). Jesus's teaching had authority because it had come directly from God.

Spending time with God on his mountain is transforming. When Moses came off the mountain of God, his face shone in radiance, so much so that he had to put a veil over his face to keep from frightening the Israelites (2 Cor 3:13). Even a short moment with God is transforming. That is why, I am sure, Jesus prayed often throughout the day when he did not have time to go up on a mountain (Luke 5:16).

When we spend time with our amazingly beautiful Lord Jesus, we too will glow. Perhaps not in the same way Moses did, but glow we will. "And we, who with unveiled faces all reflect the

Lord's glory, are being transformed into his likeness with ever-increasing glory, which comes from the Lord who is the Spirit" (2 Cor 3:18).

And we do not have to make it happen by ourselves. It is really not us at all. It is not in some feigned smile we contrive to prove our faith. It is not in the greatness of our own faith; it is in our minimum faith—our mustard-seed faith (Matt 17:20). It is only from the Spirit. "We are being transformed." You have to go to God to get it. You can get it nowhere else. "All this is from the Spirit." It is his glow we reflect when we dare "behold" him— meet him—on his mountain. We do not veil our faces, though. We are unashamed, because his grace makes us unashamed—"I am not ashamed of the gospel" (Rom 1:16). He wants others to see his glow on our faces—for us to "be aglow with the Spirit" (Rom 12:11, Revised Standard Version).

However, you do have to come down, you know. I have made many trips to the mountains of Colorado. I have had some incredible spiritual experiences there. Life is not lived there, though, for most of us. We live mostly in the valleys and flatlands where the crops grow—where our lives are meant to be lived. It is where the fields are white to harvest, as Jesus said (Matt 9:37–38). An eternal mountaintop Sabbath is coming for those who keep their eyes peeled there and are ready for him, though.

Sadly, coming off the mountain with God can be disappointing. Moses came down from Mount Sinai to an idolatrous festival. "Go down, because your people, whom you brought up out of Egypt, have become corrupt. They have been quick to turn away from what I commanded them and have made themselves an idol cast in the shape of a calf. They have bowed down to it and sacrificed to it" (Exod 32:7–8). Moses had to go down. It is disappointing at times. Disillusioning.

Elijah had to go down from his mountaintop experience. His time on the mountain had surely not been as comforting and perhaps serene as that of Moses, but it was a time of great victory—a time of destiny for him, really. However, after his great mountaintop experience, the evil Jezebel and her husband, Ahab, purposed to kill him. Elijah ran out into the desert, and sadly, he prayed to God that he might just die. But "to die is gain." Despair often follows the mountaintop. The valley is that way. Elijah: "I have had enough, Lord. Take my life; I am no better than my ancestors" (1 Kgs 19:4).

There is a poem I became acquainted with many years ago. In fact, it was a poem God used in my own calling from a purely secular career into his service. It was called "Obedience," and the first four lines are:

> *I said, "Let me walk in the fields,"*
> *He said, "No, walk in the town,"*
> *I said, "There are no flowers there,"*
> *He said, "No flowers, but a crown."*

I recently had a call from a friend whose daughter had just returned from a mission trip—her own mountaintop experience. She was down. She missed the Christian friends she had bonded so closely with there. She missed the perfect sense of purpose she had felt in such close communion with her Lord. She too had to come down, though. But she now knows where the real mountain is. And she can go back there regularly to gain the strength and energy she needs to plow the fields and plant the seed in the valley.

We go up in order to come down. "All authority in heaven and on earth has been given to me," Jesus said (Matt 28:18). He has authority on the mountaintop. He has authority in the valley too.

"Therefore go" (Matt 28:19). Go down into the valleys where the people live. Go into the shadows and bring his radiance that shows on your face. It glows because of him, not because of you! Go down and bring the healing waters of the river that flows from within you. It flows from him, not from you!

Show people where the mountain of God is. "Make disciples of all nations" (Matt 28:19). Teach them to follow him, and he will lead them to the mountain.

> In the last days the mountain of the Lord's temple will be established as chief among the mountains; it will be raised above the hills, and all nations will stream to it. Many peoples will come and say, "Come, let us go up to the mountain of the Lord, to the house of the God of Jacob. He will teach us his ways, so that we may walk in his paths." (Isa 2:2–3)

Jesus will speak to them. "His sheep follow him because they know his voice" (John 10:4).

Immerse them into him, "baptizing them in the name of the Father and of the Son and of the Holy Spirit" (Matt 28:19). Let them experience "the washing of rebirth and renewal by the Holy Spirit" (Titus 3:5). The healing waters of rebirth are for all who believe (John 1:12). And you carry the offer in your heart to all people. "You show that you are a letter from Christ...written not with ink but with the Spirit of the living God, not on tablets of stone but on tablets of human hearts" (2 Cor 3:3).

"[Teach] them to obey everything I have commanded you" (Matt 28:20). "Everyone who hears these words of mine and puts them into practice is like a wise man" (Matt 7:24). Teach those in the valley to be wise enough not only to hear but to obey. And not the rules of humanity, but the authentic words of Christ (Matt 15:1–6).

"Surely I will be with you always, to the very end of the age" (Matt 28:20). Good news—he is also in the valley with you. You can confidently go down now, because it is he who is going with you. In him you are safe because he is always near (Phil. 4:5). So go.

Reflections:

1. Something to ask: What must I grow most in to leave the mountain and go to the people God is seeking?
2. Something to think about: I can climb the mountain of God any time I wish.
3. Something to believe: God wants you to be with him. He wants to be with you.
4. Something to pray: Lord, help me to live ever near you. Help me to claim the promise of Christ of his presence in my life as I live out his mission.
5. Something to memorize: "When Jesus had finished saying these things, the crowds were amazed at his teaching, because he taught as one who had authority, and not as their teachers of the law" (Matt 7:28–29).
6. Something to do: Go down the mountain aglow with the Spirit of God. Let your light shine so that others will see your life and give glory to God (Matt 5:14–16).